Three Victorian Poets

Edited by Jane Ogborn

Series Editor: Judith Baxter

CAMBRIDGE
UNIVERSITY PRESS

PUBLISHED BY THE PRESS SYNDICATE OF THE UNIVERSITY OF CAMBRIDGE
The Pitt Building, Trumpington Street, Cambridge, United Kingdom

CAMBRIDGE UNIVERSITY PRESS
The Edinburgh Building, Cambridge CB2 2RU, UK
40 West 20th Street, New York, NY 10011–4211, USA
477 Williamstown Road, Port Melbourne, VIC 3207, Australia
Ruiz de Alarcón 13, 28014 Madrid, Spain
Dock House, The Waterfront, Cape Town 8001, South Africa

http://www.cambridge.org

This edition first published 1998
Fifth printing 2003

Printed in the United Kingdom at the University Press, Cambridge

Typeset in Sabon and Meta

A catalogue record for this book is available from the British Library

ISBN 0 521 62710 9 paperback

Prepared for publication by Stenton Associates

CONTENTS

Robert Browning

CAMBRIDGE LITERATURE

This edition of *Three Victorian Poets* is part of the Cambridge Literature series, and has been specially prepared for students in schools and colleges who are studying these poets as part of their English course.

This study edition invites you to think about what happens when you read a poem, and it suggests that you are not passively responding to words on the page which have only one agreed interpretation, but that you are actively exploring and making new sense of what you read. Your 'reading' will partly stem from you as an individual, from your own experiences and point of view, and to this extent your interpretation will be distinctively your own. But your reading will also stem from the fact that you belong to a culture and a community, rooted in a particular time and place. So, your understanding may have much in common with that of others in your class or study group.

There is a parallel between the way you read these poems and the way they were written. The Resource Notes are devised to help you to investigate the complex nature of the writing process. This begins with the poet's first, tentative ideas and sources of inspiration, moves through to the stages of writing, production and publication, and ends with the text's reception by the reading public, reviewers, critics and students. So the general approach to study focuses on five key questions:

Who has written these poems and why?

What type of texts are these poems?

How were these poems produced?

How do these poets present their subjects?

Who reads these poems? How do they interpret them?

The Resource Notes encourage you to take an active and imaginative approach to studying poetry both in and out of the classroom. As well as providing you with information about many aspects of the poets, they offer a wide choice of activities to work on individually, or in groups. Above all, they give you the chance to explore this fascinating collection in a variety of ways: as a reader, an actor, a researcher, a critic, and a writer.

Judith Baxter

INTRODUCTION

What comes into your mind when the word 'Victorian' is used? The poems in this collection have been chosen as an introduction to Victorian poetry. In the case of this anthology, the word is used to describe selections from the work of three poets whose lives between them spanned almost the whole of the nineteenth century and the reign of Queen Victoria: Alfred Tennyson (1809–1892), Elizabeth Barrett Browning (1806–1861) and Robert Browning (1812–1889). All three made their livings by writing poetry. All three were acknowledged by their contemporaries to be important poets, although they were not always unanimously admired. Since their deaths their popularity with readers has varied, but they are all recognised as contributors to the English 'literary heritage'.

A label like 'Victorian' is deceptively simple. The nineteenth century in England was a time of social upheaval, as the country became more and more industrialised, and contrasts between country and town, working class and middle class, poverty and wealth became more pronounced. It was also a time of great intellectual challenge: the discoveries of scientists like the geologist Charles Lyell (1797–1875) and the biologist Charles Darwin (1809–1882), and their theories about the origins of the human species, caused some people to question previously firm religious beliefs. It was a century of enormous energy and change, as the British Empire and British trade covered more and more of the globe.

The Time Line on pages 156–159 sets the dates of publication of the poems chosen in this collection in the context of the main political events in England and Europe, and also in relation to the publication of other significant works, especially novels. Victorian novels, rather than poetry, tend to give information and insights into people's daily life but it is difficult for a reader today to imagine what it would have been like to live 150 years ago. It may help you to understand something of the limitations, and also of the complexities, of the word 'Victorian' if you consider the social, political, economic and personal associations that a term like 'Thatcherism' has for people living at the end of the twentieth century. In the same way, the impact of Darwin on his contemporaries might be a little easier to grasp if you think about the attitudes of certain religious fundamentalists, who want to make the teaching of evolutionary theories illegal in schools, because they find these threatening to their interpretation of the Bible.

Victorian readers of poetry had a clear view of the poet's role in society. These quotations from reviews of Tennyson's *Poems* of 1842 give us some insights into what they thought poetry and the poet should be and do:

> Poetry is utterance; it is man speaking to man, man telling man his thoughts and feelings. Speech can never be long without having a direct moral character.
>
> > (Francis Garden: review in the *Christian Remembrancer*, 1842)

> [Tennyson's] command of diction is complete, his sense of execution and of the harmonies of verse accurate and admirable; he has only to show that he … comprehends the function of the poet in this day of ours, to teach still more than he delights, and to suggest still more than he teaches.
>
> > (Richard Monckton Milnes: review of second edition of *Poems* 1842, 1843)

This may suggest a quite different status and role for poets from the ones most people expect them to fulfil today. Which parts of these statements do you think still apply, and which do you think are no longer important or relevant?

One of the problems in selecting poems for this collection is that definitions of poetry, and readers' tastes, change. One example of this is that readers today (or listeners, or viewers, for that matter) are generally not very tolerant of length. Victorian readers seem to have positively welcomed it, in poetry as well as in prose.

The length of much Victorian poetry, combined with the variety of forms and genres used by poets, can make readers today think again about how they read poems. Since early in the twentieth century, poetry seems to have become defined more and more as the lyric (a short poem expressing the poet's personal thoughts and feelings). This kind of poem has taught people to become careful readers of its compressed language and its often rich associations and imagery. Long nineteenth-century poems, like Tennyson's 'Morte d'Arthur' or *Maud*, Elizabeth Barrett Browning's 'The Runaway Slave at Pilgrim's Point' or Robert Browning's 'Childe Roland to the Dark Tower Came', deserve careful readers as well. But because they also tell stories and conjure up places and people it is possible to read them in a more relaxed way, almost like short stories. The strong narrative elements, the evocative language and the rhythms the poets use can all help readers today to cope with, and enjoy, the poems' unusual length, which may initially be rather daunting. When you read these poems for the first time, go for the stories and try not to let the unfamiliar words or references and long, complicated sentences put you off. You may find that reading it aloud makes the poem a lot clearer; otherwise, try making a guess or asking a friend before you turn to the Glossary or a dictionary.

At first you may be tempted to group these three Victorian poets together and see their work as very similar, but reading and re-reading, comparing and contrasting these poems should help you to see what distinguishes one writer from another, and what the particular characteristics of each poet's work are.

✦ *Pre-reading activities*

1a   Before starting to read the poems, in a small group think about the poetry you have read which has been written during the last eighty years. Based on that reading, write your own definition of what makes poetry different from prose or drama. You might discuss: subject matter, use of rhyme, rhythm, form, length and kinds of language.

b   You have probably already read some Victorian poetry. Using that reading and the same headings, make a list of what you expect Victorian poetry to be like.

2   The Victorians are still very much part of people's lives today. Politicians talk about 'Victorian values'; in most towns, public buildings and houses dating from the nineteenth century are still in use; advertising agencies, interior decorators and the makers of greetings cards plunder the Victorian period for ideas and quotations. Do some research to find out more about what the Victorians have left behind them.

a   While you are working on these poems, you might keep a Victorian scrapbook, or build up a wall display, of:
   • pictures and images which sum up the period for you
   • allusions to the Victorian period in things you see around you
   • references in newspapers and magazines
   • references in your general reading and viewing.

b   Either look at Victorian buildings and paintings in the area where you live, or use books, reproductions and photographs to build up some familiarity with the art and architecture of the period. Depending on where you live, buildings worth looking at might include the town hall, public library, hospital, schools, churches, banks and factories. In large art galleries, some names to look for are:
   • Edward Burne-Jones (1833–1898)
   • William Holman Hunt (1827–1910)
   • John Everett Millais (1829–1896)
   • Dante Gabriel Rossetti (1828–1882)
   • John William Waterhouse (1849–1917).
   Some architects to look for are:
   • Charles Barry (1795–1860) and Augustus Welby Pugin (1812–1852), who designed the Houses of Parliament
   • William Butterfield (1814–1900)
   • William Burges (1827–1881).

*Please note that where you find * * * * * * in the text, this means that a lengthy description or the repetition of an idea has been cut to maintain the flow of the poem.*

Alfred, Lord Tennyson (1809–1892)

During his lifetime Tennyson was recognised by his contemporaries as one of England's major poets, and this status was publicly confirmed in 1850 when Queen Victoria made him the Poet Laureate. His poetry was widely read, and encompasses much that is typical of the Victorian period: the love of story, especially stories from the past, the romantic representations of women, and of men's attitudes to them, and the love of decoration, evident in the vividness and detail of his descriptions. He wrote movingly and personally about death and bereavement, and as Poet Laureate he was a patriotic but also critical spokesman for the nation. He experimented constantly with poetic forms, rhythms and language. A striking feature of many of his poems is the way in which he is able to choose and use words so that sounds and meaning echo and reinforce each other.

Break, Break, Break (1834)
In the Valley of Cauteretz (1852)

These poems were written many years apart; the first in 1834, the year after the death of Tennyson's great friend, Arthur Hallam, and the second in 1852. As young men Tennyson and Hallam had travelled together to Cauteretz, in Spain.

The length of the poems is not characteristic, but the themes and tone of the poems are. Having read them, what themes do you expect to find recurring in Tennyson's poetry?

Break, Break, Break

Break, break, break,
   On thy cold gray stones, O Sea!
And I would that my tongue could utter
   The thoughts that arise in me.

O well for the fisherman's boy,   5
   That he shouts with his sister at play!
O well for the sailor lad,
   That he sings in his boat on the bay!

And the stately ships go on
   To their haven under the hill;   10
But O for the touch of a vanish'd hand,
   And the sound of a voice that is still!

Break, break, break,
   At the foot of thy crags, O sea!
But the tender grace of a day that is dead   15
   Will never come back to me.

In the Valley of Cauteretz

All along the valley, stream that flashest white,
Deepening thy voice with the deepening of the night,
All along the valley, where thy waters flow,
I walk'd with one I loved two and thirty years ago.
All along the valley, while I walk'd to-day,   5
The two and thirty years were a mist that rolls away;
For all along the valley, down thy rocky bed,
Thy living voice to me was as the voice of the dead,
And all along the valley, by rock and cave and tree,
The voice of the dead was a living voice to me.   10

Mariana (1830)
The Sleeping Palace, The Sleeping Beauty,
The Revival (from: *The Daydream* 1834)
The Lady of Shalott (1832)
Morte d'Arthur (1834)
Ulysses (1834)

This group of poems shows Tennyson as a storyteller, using as his sources fairy tales, legends, and one of William Shakespeare's plays, all of which would have been familiar to his Victorian readers.

The extracts based on the story of the Sleeping Beauty come from a longer poem, called *The Daydream*. Tennyson has taken the idea for 'Mariana' from Shakespeare's *Measure for Measure*, making a minor character from the play into the focus of his poem. It isn't necessary to know Shakespeare's play before you can understand the poem, but if you want to compare how the two different writers use Mariana's story, you will find Shakespeare's version towards the end of Act III Scene 1, in the conversation between the Duke and Isabella. The story of the Lady of Shalott is Tennyson's own invention.

✦ *Activities*

1 Write the prose version of one of the poems, using not more than forty words. In a small group, compare your versions and discuss what you have been able to include from the poem, and what you have had to leave out.

2 Imagine you are Tennyson. An interviewer has asked you why you decided to write poems based on stories people already know. Explain what you were trying to do in each poem, apart from just retelling a story, and talk about the opportunities you think this has given you as a poet. Make sure you use plenty of examples from the poems to illustrate your answer.

Mariana

'Mariana in the moated grange.' *Measure for Measure*

With blackest moss the flower-plots
    Were thickly crusted, one and all:
The rusted nails fell from the knots
    That held the pear to the gable-wall.
The broken sheds look'd sad and strange: 5
    Unlifted was the clinking latch;
    Weeded and worn the ancient thatch
Upon the lonely moated grange.[◇]
        She only said, 'My life is dreary,
           He cometh not,' she said;   10
        She said, 'I am aweary, aweary,
           I would that I were dead!'

Her tears fell with the dews at even;
    Her tears fell ere the dews were dried;
She could not look on the sweet heaven,   15
    Either at morn or eventide.
After the flitting of the bats,
    When thickest dark did trance the sky,
    She drew her casement-curtain by,
And glanced athwart[◇] the glooming flats.[◇]   20
        She only said, 'The night is dreary,
           He cometh not,' she said;
        She said, 'I am aweary, aweary,
           I would that I were dead!'

Upon the middle of the night,   25
    Waking she heard the night-fowl crow;
The cock sung out an hour ere light:
    From the dark fen[◇] the oxen's low
Came to her: without hope of change,
    In sleep she seem'd to walk forlorn,   30

Till cold winds woke the gray-eyed morn
About the lonely moated grange.
>   She only said, 'The day is dreary,
>   He cometh not,' she said;
>   She said, 'I am aweary, aweary,   35
>   I would that I were dead!'

About a stone-cast from the wall
    A sluice with blacken'd waters slept,
And o'er it many, round and small,
    The cluster'd marish-mosses✧ crept.   40
Hard by a poplar shook alway,
    All silver-green with gnarled bark:
    For leagues no other tree did mark
The level waste, the rounding gray.
>   She only said, 'My life is dreary,   45
>   He cometh not,' she said;
>   She said, 'I am aweary, aweary,
>   I would that I were dead!'

And ever when the moon was low,
    And the shrill winds were up and away,   50
In the white curtain, to and fro,
    She saw the gusty shadow sway.
But when the moon was very low,
    And wild winds bound within their cell,
    The shadow of the poplar fell   55
Upon her bed, across her brow.
>   She only said, 'The night is dreary,
>   He cometh not,' she said;
>   She said, 'I am aweary, aweary,
>   I would that I were dead!'   60

All day within the dreamy house,
    The doors upon their hinges creak'd;
The blue fly sung in the pane; the mouse
    Behind the mouldering wainscot✧ shriek'd,
Or from the crevice peer'd about.   65

Old faces glimmer'd thro' the doors,
   Old footsteps trod the upper floors,
Old voices called her from without.
      She only said, 'My life is dreary,
         He cometh not,' she said;   70
      She said, 'I am aweary, aweary,
         I would that I were dead!'

The sparrow's chirrup on the roof,
   The slow clock ticking, and the sound
Which to the wooing wind aloof   75
   The poplar made, did all confound
Her sense; but most she loathed the hour
   When the thick-moted◇ sunbeam lay
   Athwart the chambers, and the day
Was sloping toward his western bower.   80
      Then, said she, 'I am very dreary,
         He will not come,' she said;
      She wept, 'I am aweary, aweary,
         Oh God, that I were dead!'

from *The Daydream*

The Sleeping Palace

I

The varying year with blade and sheaf
    Clothes and reclothes the happy plains,
Here rests the sap within the leaf,
    Here stays the blood along the veins.
Faint shadows, vapours lightly curl'd,   5
    Faint murmurs from the meadows come,
Like hints and echoes of the world
    To spirits folded in the womb.

II

Soft lustre bathes the range of urns
    On every slanting terrace-lawn.   10
The fountain to his place returns
    Deep in the garden lake withdrawn.
Here droops the banner on the tower,
    On the hall-hearths the festal fires,
The peacock in his laurel bower,   15
    The parrot in his gilded wires.

III

Roof-haunting martins warm their eggs:
    In these, in those the life is stay'd.
The mantles° from the golden pegs
    Droop sleepily: no sound is made,   20
Not even of a gnat that sings.
    More like a picture seemeth all
Than those old portraits of old kings,
    That watch the sleepers from the wall.

IV

Here sits the Butler with a flask   25
    Between his knees, half drain'd; and there
The wrinkled steward at his task,
    The maid-of-honour blooming fair;
The page has caught her hand in his:
    Her lips are sever'd as to speak: 30
His own are pouted to a kiss:
    The blush is fix'd upon her cheek.

V

Till all the hundred summers pass,
    The beams, that thro' the Oriel◊ shine,
Make prisms in every carven glass,   35
    And beaker brimm'd with noble wine.
Each baron at the banquet sleeps,
    Grave faces gather'd in a ring.
His state the king reposing keeps.
    He must have been a jovial king.   40

VI

All round a hedge upshoots, and shows
    At distance like a little wood;
Thorns, ivies, woodbine, mistletoes,
    And grapes with bunches red as blood;
All creeping plants, a wall of green   45
    Close-matted, bur and brake◊ and briar
And glimpsing over these, just seen,
    High up, the topmost palace spire.

VII

When will the hundred summers die,
    And thought and time be born again,   50
And newer knowledge, drawing nigh,
    Bring truth that sways the soul of men?
Here all things in their place remain,
    As all were order'd, ages since.
Come, Care and Pleasure, Hope and Pain,   55
    And bring the fated fairy Prince.

The Sleeping Beauty

I

Year after year unto her feet,
    She lying on her couch alone,
Across the purple coverlet,
    The maiden's jet-black hair has grown,
On either side her tranced form   5
    Forth streaming from a braid of pearl:
The slumbrous light is rich and warm,
    And moves not on the rounded curl.

II

The silk star-broider'd coverlid
    Unto her limbs itself doth mould   10
Languidly ever; and, amid
    Her full black ringlets downward roll'd,
Glows forth each softly-shadow'd arm
    With bracelets of the diamond bright:
Her constant beauty doth inform   15
    Stillness with love, and day with light.

III

She sleeps: her breathings are not heard
    In palace chambers far apart.
The fragrant tresses are not stirr'd
    That lie upon her charmed heart.   20
She sleeps: on either hand upswells
    The gold-fringed pillow lightly prest:
She sleeps, nor dreams, but ever dwells
    A perfect form in perfect rest.

The Revival

I

A touch, a kiss! the charm was snapt.
    There rose a noise of striking clocks,
And feet that ran, and doors that clapt,
    And barking dogs, and crowing cocks;
A fuller light illumined all,   5
    A breeze thro' all the garden swept,
A sudden hubbub shook the hall,
    And sixty feet the fountain leapt.

II

The hedge broke in, the banner blew,
    The butler drank, the steward scrawl'd,   10
The fire shot up, the martin flew,
    The parrot scream'd, the peacock squall'd,
The maid and page renew'd their strife,
    The palace bang'd, and buzz'd and clackt,
And all the long-pent stream of life   15
    Dash'd downward in a cataract.◇

The Lady of Shalott

Part I

On either side the river lie
Long fields of barley and of rye,
That clothe the wold◇ and meet the sky;
And thro' the field the road runs by
 To many-tower'd Camelot;   5
And up and down the people go,
Gazing where the lilies blow
Round an island there below,
 The island of Shalott.

Willows whiten, aspens quiver,   10
Little breezes dusk and shiver
Thro' the wave that runs for ever
By the island in the river
 Flowing down to Camelot.
Four gray walls, and four gray towers,   15
Overlook a space of flowers,
And the silent isle imbowers
 The Lady of Shalott.

By the margin, willow-veil'd,
Slide the heavy barges trail'd   20
By slow horses; and unhail'd
The shallop◇ flitteth silken-sail'd
 Skimming down to Camelot:
But who hath seen her wave her hand?
Or at the casement seen her stand?   25
Or is she known in all the land,
 The Lady of Shalott?

Only reapers, reaping early
In among the bearded barley,
Hear a song that echoes cheerly   30

From the river winding clearly,
　　Down to tower'd Camelot:
And by the moon the reaper weary,
Piling sheaves in uplands airy,
Listening, whispers, ''Tis the fairy　　　　　　　　35
　　Lady of Shalott.'

Part II
There she weaves by night and day
A magic web with colours gay.
She has heard a whisper say,
A curse is on her if she stay[◇]　　　　　　　40
　　To look down to Camelot.
She knows not what the curse may be,
And so she weaveth steadily,
And little other care hath she,
　　The Lady of Shalott.　　　　　　　　　　　45

And moving thro' a mirror clear
That hangs before her all the year,
Shadows of the world appear.
There she sees the highway near
　　Winding down to Camelot:　　　　　　　　50
There the river eddy whirls,
And there the surly village-churls,
And the red cloaks of market girls,
　　Pass onward from Shalott.

Sometimes a troop of damsels glad,　　　　　55
An abbot on an ambling pad,[◇]
Sometimes a curly shepherd-lad,
Or long-hair'd page in crimson clad,
　　Goes by to tower'd Camelot;
And sometimes thro' the mirror blue　　　　60
The knights come riding two and two:
She hath no loyal knight and true,
　　The Lady of Shalott.

But in her web she still delights
To weave the mirror's magic sights,   65
For often thro' the silent nights
A funeral, with plumes and lights
   And music, went to Camelot:
Or when the moon was overhead,
Came two young lovers lately wed;   70
'I am half sick of shadows,' said
   The Lady of Shalott.

Part III

A bow-shot from her bower-eaves,
He rode between the barley-sheaves,
The sun came dazzling thro' the leaves,   75
And flamed upon the brazen greaves◊
   Of bold Sir Lancelot.
A red-cross knight for ever kneel'd
To a lady in his shield,
That sparkled on the yellow field,   80
   Beside remote Shalott.

The gemmy bridle glitter'd free,
Like to some branch of stars we see
Hung in the golden Galaxy.
The bridle bells rang merrily   85
   As he rode down to Camelot:
And from his blazon'd baldric◊ slung
A mighty silver bugle hung,
And as he rode his armour rung,
   Beside remote Shalott.   90

All in the blue unclouded weather
Thick-jewell'd shone the saddle-leather,
The helmet and the helmet-feather
Burn'd like one burning flame together,
   As he rode down to Camelot.   95
As often thro' the purple night,
Below the starry clusters bright,

Some bearded meteor, trailing light,
 Moves over still Shalott.

His broad clear brow in sunlight glow'd;   100
On burnish'd hooves his war-horse trode;
From underneath his helmet flow'd
His coal-black curls as on he rode,
 As he rode down to Camelot.
From the bank and from the river   105
He flash'd into the crystal mirror,
'Tirra lirra,' by the river
 Sang Sir Lancelot.

She left the web, she left the loom,
She made three paces thro' the room,   110
She saw the water-lily bloom,
She saw the helmet and the plume,
 She look'd down to Camelot.
Out flew the web and floated wide;
The mirror crack'd from side to side;   115
'The curse is come upon me,' cried
 The Lady of Shalott.

Part IV
In the stormy east-wind straining,
The pale yellow woods were waning,
The broad stream in his banks complaining,   120
Heavily the low sky raining
 Over tower'd Camelot;
Down she came and found a boat
Beneath a willow left afloat,
And round about the prow she wrote   125
 The Lady of Shalott.

And down the river's dim expanse
Like some bold seër in a trance,
Seeing all his own mischance –
With a glassy countenance   130

Did she look to Camelot.
And at the closing of the day
She loosed the chain, and down she lay;
The broad stream bore her far away,
   The Lady of Shalott.   135

Lying, robed in snowy white
That loosely flew to left and right –
The leaves upon her falling light –
Thro' the noises of the night
   She floated down to Camelot: 140
And as the boat-head wound along
The willowy hills and fields among,
They heard her singing her last song,
   The Lady of Shalott.

Heard a carol, mournful, holy,   145
Chanted loudly, chanted lowly,
Till her blood was frozen slowly,
And her eyes were darken'd wholly,
   Turn'd to tower'd Camelot.
For ere she reach'd upon the tide   150
The first house by the water-side,
Singing in her song she died,
   The Lady of Shalott.

Under tower and balcony,
By garden-wall and gallery,   155
A gleaming shape she floated by,
Dead-pale between the houses high,
   Silent into Camelot.
Out upon the wharfs they came,
Knight and burgher, lord and dame,   160
And round the prow they read her name,
   The Lady of Shalott.

Who is this? and what is here?
And in the lighted palace near
Died the sound of royal cheer;   165
And they cross'd themselves for fear,
    All the knights at Camelot:
But Lancelot mused a little space;
He said, 'She has a lovely face;
God in his mercy lend her grace,   170
    The Lady of Shalott.'

Morte d'Arthur

Tennyson based his version of the death of Arthur on the story of King Arthur by the fifteenth-century writer, Sir Thomas Malory. Tennyson first wrote this poem in 1834. Thirty-five years later he included it in *The Idylls of the King*, his retelling of the stories of King Arthur and the knights of the Round Table. He gave it a new title, 'The passing of Arthur', but otherwise left the poem unaltered.

'Idyllic' means 'wonderfully peaceful and happy'; an 'idyll' is writing which describes peaceful, happy scenes. It is a strange term for Tennyson to use for long, narrative poems about the court of King Arthur, which deal with heroism, relationships between men and women and struggles between good and evil – themes and ways of writing about them more often referred to in literature as 'epic'.

✦ *Activities*

1 Read both versions of the story. How has Tennyson used Malory's version? What additions and alterations has he made to it? Why do you think he has made them?

2 Tennyson dedicated *The Idylls of the King* to Queen Victoria and Prince Albert, comparing both of them to King Arthur himself in the short poems he placed at the beginning and the end of the collection of stories. This would obviously appeal to the Queen, but what do you find in this poem:
   • which you think would appeal to other Victorian readers?
   • which makes it worth reading today?

From *Morte d'Arthur* by Sir Thomas Malory

'Therefore' said Arthur unto Sir Bedevere, 'take thou Excalibur, my good sword and go with it to yonder water side, and when thou comest there I charge thee throw my sword in that water, and come again and tell me what thou there seest.'

'My lord,' said Bedevere, 'your commandment shall be 5 done, and lightly bring you word again.'

So Sir Bedevere departed, and by the way he beheld that noble sword, that the pommel and the haft was all of precious stones; and then he said to himself, 'If I throw this rich sword in the water, thereof shall never come good, but harm and 10 loss.' And then Sir Bedevere hid Excalibur under a tree.

And so, as soon as he might, he came again unto the king, and said he had been at the water, and had thrown the sword in the water.

'What saw thou there?' said the king. 15

'Sir,' he said, 'I saw nothing but waves and winds.'

'That is untruly said of thee,' said the king, 'therefore go thou lightly again, and do my commandment; as thou art to me leve° and dear, spare not, but throw it in.'

Then Sir Bedevere returned again, and took the sword in his 20 hand; and then him thought sin and shame to throw away that noble sword, and so eft° he hid the sword, and returned again, and told to the king that he had been at the water and done his commandment.

'What saw thou there?' said the king. 25

'Sir,' he said, 'I saw nothing but the waters wap and the waves wan.'

'Ah, traitor untrue' said King Arthur, 'now hast thou betrayed me twice. Who would have weened° that thou that hast been to me so leve and dear, and thou art named a noble 30 knight, and would betray me for the riches of the sword? But now go again lightly, for thy long tarrying putteth me in great jeopardy of my life, for I have taken cold. And but if thou do now as I bid thee, if ever I may see thee, I shall slay thee with

mine own hands; for thou wouldst for my rich sword see me 35
dead.'

Then Sir Bedevere departed, and went to the sword, and
lightly took it up, and went to the water side; and there he
bound the girdle about the hilts, and then he threw the sword
as far into the water as he might; and there came an arm and an 40
hand above the water and met it, and caught it, and so shook it
thrice and brandished, and then vanished away the hand with
the sword in the water.

So Sir Bedevere came again to the king, and told him what
he saw. 45

'Alas,' said the king, 'help me hence, for I dread me I have
tarried◦ over long.'

Then Sir Bedevere took the king upon his back, and so went
with him to that water side. And when they were at the water
side, even fast by the bank hoved a little barge with many fair 50
ladies in it, and among them all was a queen, and all they had
black hoods, and all they wept and shrieked when they saw
King Arthur.

'Now put me into the barge,' said the king.

And so he did softly; and there received him three queens 55
with great mourning; and so they set them down, and in one of
their laps King Arthur laid his head.

And then that queen said, 'Ah, dear brother, why have ye
tarried so long from me? Alas, this wound on your head hath
caught over-much cold.' 60

And so then they rowed from the land, and Sir Bedevere
beheld all those ladies go from him.

Then Sir Bedevere cried, 'Ah my lord Arthur, what shall
become of me, now ye go from me and leave me here alone
among mine enemies?' 65

'Comfort thyself', said the king, 'and do as well as thou
mayest, for in me is no trust for to trust in; for I will into the
vale of Avilion to heal me of my grievous wound; and if thou
hear never more of me, pray for my soul.'

But ever the queens and ladies wept and shrieked, that it 70
was pity to hear. And as soon as Sir Bedevere had lost sight of
the barge, he wept and wailed, and so took to the forest.

Morte d'Arthur

So all day long the noise of battle roll'd
Among the mountains by the winter sea;
Until King Arthur's Table, man by man,
Had fall'n in Lyonnesse about their lord,
King Arthur. Then, because his wound was deep,   5
The bold Sir Bedivere uplifted him,
And bore him to a chapel nigh the field,
A broken chancel with a broken cross,
That stood on a dark strait of barren land:
On one side lay the Ocean, and on one   10
Lay a great water, and the moon was full.

   Then spake King Arthur to Sir Bedivere:
'The sequel of to-day unsolders[◇] all
The goodliest fellowship of famous knights
Whereof this world holds record. Such a sleep   15
They sleep – the men I loved. I think that we
Shall never more, at any future time,
Delight our souls with talk of knightly deeds,
Walking about the gardens and the halls
Of Camelot, as in the days that were.   20
I perish by this people which I made, –
Tho' Merlin[◇] sware that I should come again
To rule once more; but, let what will be, be,
I am so deeply smitten thro' the helm
That without help I cannot last till morn.   25
Thou therefore take my brand[◇] Excalibur,
Which was my pride: for thou rememberest how
In those old days, one summer noon, an arm
Rose up from out the bosom of the lake,
Clothed in white samite,[◇] mystic, wonderful,   30
Holding the sword – and how I row'd across
And took it, and have worn it, like a king;
And, wheresoever I am sung or told

In aftertime, this also shall be known:
But now delay not: take Excalibur,   35
And fling him far into the middle mere:◇
Watch what thou seëst, and lightly◇ bring me word.'

   To him replied the bold Sir Bedivere:
'It is not meet, Sir King, to leave thee thus,
Aidless, alone, and smitten thro' the helm –   40
A little thing may harm a wounded man;
Yet I thy hest◇ will all perform at full,
Watch what I see, and lightly bring thee word.'

   So saying, from the ruin'd shrine he stept,
And in the moon athwart the place of tombs,   45
Where lay the mighty bones of ancient men,
Old knights, and over them the sea-wind sang
Shrill, chill, with flakes of foam. He, stepping down
By zigzag paths and juts of pointed rock,
Came on the shining levels of the lake.   50

   There drew he forth the brand Excalibur,
And o'er him, drawing it, the winter moon,
Brightening the skirts of a long cloud, ran forth
And sparkled keen with frost against the hilt:
For all the haft twinkled with diamond sparks,   55
Myriads of topaz-lights, and jacinth-work
Of subtlest jewellery. He gazed so long
That both his eyes were dazzled as he stood,
This way and that dividing the swift mind,
In act to throw: but at the last it seem'd   60
Better to leave Excalibur conceal'd
There in the many-knotted waterflags,◇
That whistled stiff and dry about the marge.◇
So strode he back slow to the wounded King.

   Then spake King Arthur to Sir Bedivere: 65
'Hast thou perform'd my mission which I gave?
What is it thou hast seen? or what hast heard?'

And answer made the bold Sir Bedivere:
'I heard the ripple washing in the reeds,
And the wild water lapping on the crag.'   70

To whom replied King Arthur, faint and pale:
'Thou hast betray'd thy nature and thy name,
Not rendering true answer, as beseem'd
Thy fëalty,◇ nor like a noble knight:
For surer sign had follow'd, either hand,   75
Or voice, or else a motion of the mere.
This is a shameful thing for men to lie.
Yet now, I charge thee, quickly go again,
As thou art lief◇ and dear, and do the thing
I bade thee, watch, and lightly bring me word.'   80

Then went Sir Bedivere the second time
Across the ridge, and paced beside the mere,
Counting the dewy pebbles, fix'd in thought;
But when he saw the wonder of the hilt,
How curiously and strangely chased,◇ he smote   85
His palms together, and he cried aloud:

'And if indeed I cast the brand away,
Surely a precious thing, one worthy note,
Should thus be lost for ever from the earth,
Which might have pleased the eyes of many men.   90
What good should follow this, if this were done?
What harm, undone? Deep harm to disobey,
Seeing obedience is the bond of rule.
Were it well to obey then, if a king demand
An act unprofitable, against himself?   95
The King is sick, and knows not what he does.
What record, or what relic of my lord
Should be to aftertime, but empty breath
And rumours of a doubt? But were this kept,
Stored in some treasure-house of mighty kings,   100
Some one might show it at a joust of arms,

31

Saying, "King Arthur's sword, Excalibur,
Wrought by the lonely maiden of the Lake.
Nine years she wrought it, sitting in the deeps
Upon the hidden bases of the hills."   105
So might some old man speak in the aftertime
To all the people, winning reverence.
But now much honour and much fame were lost.'

  So spake he, clouded with his own conceit,
And hid Excalibur the second time,   110
And so strode back slow to the wounded King.

  Then spoke King Arthur, breathing heavily:
'What is it thou hast seen? or what hast heard?'

  And answer made the bold Sir Bedivere:
'I heard the water lapping on the crag,   115
And the long ripple washing in the reeds.'

  To whom replied King Arthur, much in wrath:
'Ah, miserable and unkind, untrue,
Unknightly, traitor-hearted! Woe is me!
Authority forgets a dying king,   120
Laid widow'd of the power in his eye
That bow'd the will. I see thee what thou art,
For thou, the latest-left of all my knights,
In whom should meet the offices of all,
Thou wouldst betray me for the precious hilt;   125
Either from lust of gold, or like a girl
Valuing the giddy pleasure of the eyes.
Yet, for a man may fail in duty twice,
And the third time may prosper, get thee hence:
But, if thou spare to fling Excalibur,   130
I will arise and slay thee with my hands.'

Then quickly rose Sir Bedivere, and ran,
And, leaping down the ridges lightly, plunged
Among the bulrush beds, and clutch'd the sword,
And strongly wheel'd and threw it. The great brand   135
Made lightnings in the splendour of the moon,
And flashing round and round, and whirl'd in an arch,
Shot like a streamer of the northern morn,
Seen where the moving isles of winter shock
By night, with noises of the Northern Sea.   140
So flash'd and fell the brand Excalibur:
But ere he dipt the surface, rose an arm
Clothed in white samite, mystic, wonderful,
And caught him by the hilt, and brandish'd him
Three times, and drew him under in the mere.   145
And lightly went the other to the King.

Then spoke King Arthur, drawing thicker breath:
'Now see I by thine eyes that this is done.
Speak out: what is it thou hast heard, or seen?'

And answer made the bold Sir Bedivere: 150
'Sir King, I closed mine eyelids, lest the gems
Should blind my purpose, for I never saw,
Nor shall see, here or elsewhere, till I die,
Not tho' I live three lives of mortal men,
So great a miracle as yonder hilt.   155
Then with both hands I flung him, wheeling him;
But when I look'd again, behold an arm,
Clothed in white samite, mystic, wonderful,
That caught him by the hilt, and brandish'd him
Three times, and drew him under in the mere.'   160

And answer made King Arthur, breathing hard:
'My end draws nigh; 'tis time that I were gone.
Make broad thy shoulders to receive my weight,
And bear me to the margin; yet I fear
My wound hath taken cold, and I shall die.'   165

So saying, from the pavement he half rose,
Slowly, with pain, reclining on his arm,
And looking wistfully with wide blue eyes
As in a picture. Him Sir Bedivere
Remorsefully regarded thro' his tears,   170
And would have spoken, but he found not words;
Then took with care, and kneeling on one knee,
O'er both his shoulders drew the languid hands,
And rising bore him thro' the place of tombs.

But, as he walk'd, King Arthur panted hard,   175
Like one that feels a nightmare on his bed
When all the house is mute. So sigh'd the King,
Muttering and murmuring at his ear, 'Quick, quick!
I fear it is too late, and I shall die.'
But the other swiftly strode from ridge to ridge,   180
Clothed with his breath, and looking, as he walk'd,
Larger than human on the frozen hills.
He heard the deep behind him, and a cry
Before. His own thought drove him like a goad.
Dry clash'd his harness in the icy caves   185
And barren chasms, and all to left and right
The bare black cliff clang'd round him, as he based
His feet on juts of slippery crag that rang
Sharp-smitten with the dint of armed heels –
And on a sudden, lo! the level lake,   190
And the long glories of the winter moon.

Then saw they how there hove a dusky barge,
Dark as a funeral scarf from stem to stern,
Beneath them; and descending they were ware
That all the decks were dense with stately forms,   195
Black-stoled, black-hooded, like a dream – by these
Three Queens with crowns of gold: and from them rose
A cry that shiver'd to the tingling stars,
And, as it were one voice, an agony
Of lamentation, like a wind that shrills   200
All night in a waste land, where no one comes,
Or hath come, since the making of the world.

Then murmur'd Arthur, 'Place me in the barge.'
So to the barge they came. There those three Queens
Put forth their hands, and took the King, and wept.　　205
But she, that rose the tallest of them all
And fairest, laid his head upon her lap,
And loosed the shatter'd casque,◇ and chafed his hands,
And call'd him by his name, complaining loud,
And dropping bitter tears against a brow　　210
Striped with dark blood: for all his face was white
And colourless, and like the wither'd moon
Smote by the fresh beam of the springing east;
And all his greaves and cuisses◇ dash'd with drops
Of onset;◇ and the light and lustrous curls –　　215
That made his forehead like a rising sun
High from the daïs-throne – were parch'd with dust;
Or, clotted into points and hanging loose,
Mix'd with the knightly growth that fringed his lips.
So like a shatter'd column lay the King;　　220
Not like that Arthur who, with lance in rest,
From spur to plume a star of tournament,
Shot thro' the lists at Camelot, and charged
Before the eyes of ladies and of kings.

Then loudly cried the bold Sir Bedivere:　　225
'Ah! my Lord Arthur, whither shall I go?
Where shall I hide my forehead and my eyes?
For now I see the true old times are dead,
When every morning brought a noble chance,
And every chance brought out a noble knight.　　230
Such times have been not since the light that led
The holy Elders with the gift of myrrh.
But now the whole Round Table is dissolved
Which was an image of the mighty world,
And I, the last, go forth companionless,　　235
And the days darken round me, and the years,
Among new men, strange faces, other minds.'

And slowly answer'd Arthur from the barge:
'The old order changeth, yielding place to new,
And God fulfils himself in many ways,   240
Lest one good custom should corrupt the world.
Comfort thyself: what comfort is in me?
I have lived my life, and that which I have done
May He within himself make pure! but thou,
If thou shouldst never see my face again,   245
Pray for my soul. More things are wrought by prayer
Than this world dreams of. Wherefore, let thy voice
Rise like a fountain for me night and day.
For what are men better than sheep or goats
That nourish a blind life within the brain,   250
If, knowing God, they lift not hands of prayer
Both for themselves and those who call them friend?
For so the whole round earth is every way
Bound by gold chains about the feet of God.
But now farewell. I am going a long way   255
With these thou seëst – if indeed I go
(For all my mind is clouded with a doubt) –
To the island-valley of Avilion;◇
Where falls not hail, or rain, or any snow,
Nor ever wind blows loudly; but it lies   260
Deep-meadow'd, happy, fair with orchard lawns
And bowery hollows crown'd with summer sea,
Where I will heal me of my grievous wound.'

So said he, and the barge with oar and sail
Moved from the brink, like some full-breasted swan   265
That, fluting a wild carol ere her death,
Ruffles her pure cold plume, and takes the flood
With swarthy webs. Long stood Sir Bedivere
Revolving many memories, till the hull
Look'd one black dot against the verge of dawn,   270
And on the mere the wailing died away.

Ulysses (1834)

'Ulysses' is written in the voice of the hero of the Trojan wars, survivor of many dangers and adventures on his long journey home to Ithaca, in Greece, where he has been reunited with his wife Penelope.

◆ *Activity*

Tennyson wrote this poem in 1834, not long after the death of his friend, Arthur Hallam. Hallam was only twenty-three when he died; Tennyson was twenty-five. He said about the poem:

> There is more about myself in 'Ulysses', which was
> written under the sense of loss and that all had gone
> by, but that still life must be fought out to the end.
> It was more written with the feeling of his loss upon
> me than many poems in *In Memoriam*.

In what ways does this information about the writing of 'Ulysses' add to or alter your first reading of the poem?

Ulysses

It little profits that an idle king,
By this still hearth, among these barren crags,
Matched with an agèd wife, I mete and dole°
Unequal laws unto a savage race,
That hoard, and sleep, and feed, and know not me.   5

I cannot rest from travel; I will drink
Life to the lees.° All times I have enjoyed
Greatly, have suffered greatly, both with those
That loved me, and alone; on shore, and when
Through scudding drifts the rainy Hyades   10
Vext the dim sea: I am become a name
For always roaming with a hungry heart;
Much have I seen and known, – cities of men
And manners, climates, councils, governments,
Myself not least, but honoured of them all;   15
And drunk delight of battle with my peers,
Far on the ringing plains of windy Troy.

I am a part of all that I have met;
Yet all experience is an arch wherethrough
Gleams that untravelled world whose margin fades   20
For ever and for ever when I move.
How dull it is to pause, to make an end,
To rust unburnished, not to shine in use!
As though to breathe were life! Life piled on life
Were all too little, and of one to me   25
Little remains; but every hour is saved
From that eternal silence, something more,
A bringer of new things; and vile it were
For some three suns to store and hoard myself,
And this grey spirit yearning in desire   30
To follow knowledge like a sinking star,
Beyond the utmost bound of human thought.

This is my son, mine own Telemachus,
To whom I leave the sceptre and the isle –
Well-loved of me, discerning to fulfil   35
This labour, by slow prudence to make mild
A rugged people, and through soft degrees
Subdue them to the useful and the good.
Most blameless is he, centred in the sphere
Of common duties, decent not to fail   40
In offices of tenderness, and pay
Meet adoration to my household gods,
When I am gone. He works his work, I mine.

There lies the port; the vessel puffs her sail;
There gloom the dark, broad seas. My mariners,   45
Souls that have toiled, and wrought, and thought with me –
That ever with a frolic welcome took
The thunder and the sunshine, and opposed
Free hearts, free foreheads – you and I are old;
Old age hath yet his honour and his toil.   50
Death closes all; but something ere the end,
Some work of noble note, may yet be done,
Not unbecoming men that strove with Gods.
The lights begin to twinkle from the rocks;
The long day wanes; the slow moon climbs; the deep   55
Moans round with many voices. Come, my friends,
'Tis not too late to seek a newer world.
Push off, and sitting well in order smite
The sounding furrows; for my purpose holds
To sail beyond the sunset, and the baths   60
Of all the western stars, until I die.
It may be that the gulfs will wash us down;
It may be we shall touch the Happy Isles,
And see the great Achilles, whom we knew.
Though much is taken, much abides; and though   65

We are not now that strength which in old days
Moved earth and heaven; that which we are, we are:
One equal temper of heroic hearts,
Made weak by time and fate, but strong in will
To strive, to seek, to find, and not to yield.   70

The Princess (1847)

The Princess is more like a novel than a poem – not the sort of poetry readers are very familiar with today. Tennyson's subtitle for it, 'A Medley', seems a good description. It starts at a Victorian country house party of aristocratic young people, where a communal story-telling session is suggested. The 'story' is made up of seven sections, or chapters, interspersed with 'songs'. These are lyric poems which have often been taken out of context and put into poetry anthologies as poems in their own right.

The seven chapters tell the story of an arranged marriage between a prince and princess who have never met. The princess, a firm believer in women's rights and the importance of education, founds a university for women which men are forbidden to enter. Of course, the prince and his friends succeed in doing so, disguised as women! Inevitably they are found out; in the resulting mock heroic battle the prince is injured, and while nursing him back to health the princess falls in love. Also inevitably, the marriage takes place after all.

'Now sleeps the crimson petal' is a poem within the poem, which the princess has found in 'a volume of the Poets of her land' which she is reading at the injured prince's bedside while he is asleep.

✦ *Activities*

1 With a partner, discuss your first impressions of this poem.

2 The princess is reading the poem, she is not the writer or the speaker of it.
   a From your knowledge of anthologies of poetry, do you think the 'Poets of her land' are more likely to be men or women?
   b Does the gender of the 'speaker' affect the way you read and interpret the poem?

from *The Princess*

Now sleeps the crimson petal, now the white;
Nor waves the cypress in the palace walk;
Nor winks the gold fin in the porphyry[◇] font;
The firefly wakens: waken thou with me.

Now droops the milkwhite peacock like a ghost,   5
And like a ghost she glimmers on to me.

Now lies the Earth all Danae[◇] to the stars,
And all thy heart lies open unto me.

Now slides the silent meteor on, and leaves
A shining furrow, as thy thoughts in me.   10

Now folds the lily all her sweetness up,
And slips into the bosom of the lake:
So fold thyself, my dearest, thou, and slip
Into my bosom and be lost in me.

'Blame not thyself' (1847)

The Princess is a mixture of comedy and seriousness, but the issue of women's education, and the definition of the woman's role was of great importance to the Victorians and is a theme of many of the novels of the period, especially those written by women.

As the prince recovers, the princess struggles with her conflicting emotions and principles, and questions the effect of her efforts to achieve education and rights for women.

The extract, 'Blame not thyself', is the prince's response to her doubts about her actions and about the success of her project to give women independence.

✦ *Activity*

How does the prince see the relationship between men and women?

a Make three lists, headed: According to the prince
  - Men are ...
  - Women are ...
  - Together they ...

b What is your opinion of his views?

Blame not thyself

'Blame not thyself too much,' I said, 'nor blame
Too much the sons of men and barbarous laws;
These were the rough ways of the world till now.
Henceforth thou hast a helper, me, that know
The woman's cause is man's: they rise or sink   5
Together, dwarf'd or godlike, bond or free:
For she that out of Lethe° scales with man
The shining steps of Nature, shares with man
His nights, his days, moves with him to one goal,
Stays all the fair young planet in her hands –   10
If she be small, slight-natured, miserable,
How shall men grow? but work no more alone!
Our place is much: as far as in us lies
We two will serve them both in aiding her –
Will clear away the parasitic forms   15
That seem to keep her up but drag her down –
Will leave her space to burgeon° out of all
Within her – let her make herself her own
To give or keep, to live and learn and be
All that not harms distinctive womanhood.   20
For woman is not undevelopt man,
But diverse: could we make her as the man,
Sweet Love were slain: his dearest bond is this,
Not like to like, but like in difference.
Yet in the long years liker must they grow;   25
The man be more of woman, she of man;
He gain in sweetness and in moral height,
Nor lose the wrestling thews° that throw the world;
She mental breadth, nor fail in childward care,
Nor lose the childlike in the larger mind;   30
Till at the last she set herself to man,
Like perfect music unto noble words;
And so these twain, upon the skirts of Time,
Sit side by side, full-summ'd in all their powers,

Dispensing harvest, sowing the To-be,   35
Self-reverent each and reverencing each,
Distinct in individualities,
But like each other ev'n as those who love.
Then comes the statelier Eden back to men:
Then reign the world's great bridals, chaste and calm: 40
Then springs the crowning race of humankind.

In Memoriam (1850)

In Memoriam is not one single poem, but a sequence of one hundred and thirty-one shorter poems. These were written over a long period of time, between the death abroad of Tennyson's friend Arthur Hallam, in September 1833, and the publication of the poem in 1850 (the year in which Tennyson became the Poet Laureate). Many of the poems that make up *In Memoriam* are often anthologised out of their context, in the same way as 'Now sleeps the crimson petal' and 'Come into the garden, Maud' have been. The whole sequence is an elegy to Hallam, who was to have married Tennyson's sister Emily. In it, Tennyson explores his sense of bereavement, and his struggle to reconcile his feelings of personal loss with his religious beliefs.

Unlike *The Princess* or *Maud*, in which Tennyson uses a variety of poetic forms within the piece, all the lyrics that make up *In Memoriam* are written in the same four-line stanza, with the same scheme of rhyming for the first and last lines, and for the second and third. It is a tribute to Tennyson's skill as a poet that he can use this form so flexibly and it does not become monotonous. In fact, its repetition is one of the features of *In Memoriam* which critics often praise. Michael Wheeler (in *Death and the Future Life in Victorian Literature and Theology*, Cambridge University Press, 1990) compares the rhythms of the verse to the regular beating of the heart, with the final line lifting the verse to meet the rhyme of its opening line. Christopher Ricks (in *Tennyson*, Macmillan, 1989) describes it as:

> a stanza which rises to a momentary chime and then fades – but does not fade into despair and vacuity, only into dimness and regret, since after all there comes the distant rhyme.

Your responses to two central aspects of *In Memoriam* – male friendship and religion – are likely to have some effect on your reading of the poem. The intensity of language, which is a characteristic of Tennyson's poetry, is used here to describe his feelings about Hallam, and the friendship with him was undoubtedly extremely important to Tennyson. This may suggest a homosexual relationship to readers today, but it is important to be wary of imposing modern interpretations on nineteenth-century texts.

Although the separate poems were written at different times, the whole sequence is given an overall structure by the progress of time through the three Christmases described, the changing seasons and the development of the poet's thoughts about death, religion and his own life. Tennyson's struggle to reconcile his feelings about the loss of his friend with his belief in God is central, but readers who do not share his religious beliefs may find this struggle hard to understand fully. They may find it easier to empathise with his exploration of the different stages of his feelings about his bereavement, from the initial pain and grief to final acceptance.

The selection of poems from *In Memoriam* is in the order in which they come in the whole work. It makes use of Tennyson's own statement that the three Christmases act as markers for the different stages in the whole poem and link its otherwise loosely connected sections together. *In Memoriam* begins with a direct address to God, expressing Tennyson's faith in His will:

We have but faith: we cannot know;
   For knowledge is of things we see;
   And yet we trust it comes from thee,
A beam in darkness: let it grow.

The movement of the whole work is towards Tennyson's full expression of this belief, starting from his dreadful grief at the death of his friend.

✦ *Activities*

1 This selection presents you with a reading of *In Memoriam* which foregrounds Tennyson's emotions. As you read through the separate poems, try to sum up the feelings that he goes through. Plot the poems on an 'intensity' graph, with brief annotations, to show how the poet comes to terms with his grief and loss.

2 All the lyrics in *In Memoriam* are written in the same verse form. Look at the comments on page 47 about this verse form from two critics.

    a Discuss the ways Tennyson uses the verse, and the variations of pace and mood that you have noticed in the selection.

    b Using any of the lyrics as a model, try to write a short poem of your own using the *In Memoriam* rhythm and rhyme scheme.

3 How does the context affect the way you read a poem? Lyric CVI ('Ring out, wild bells') is often printed in anthologies as a poem in its own right.

    a When you read it in its place near the end of *In Memoriam*, and in the context of the other lyrics from it, what do you think it is about?

    b Look at the Key Events column of the Time Line (pp. 156–159). *In Memoriam* was written between 1833 and 1850. When you think about what was going on in England while Tennyson was writing, what alternative interpretations of 'Ring out, wild bells' can you suggest?

from *In Memoriam A. H. H. Obiit* MDCCCXXXIII
(In memory of Arthur Henry Hallam, died 1833)

VII

Dark house, by which once more I stand
   Here in the long unlovely street,
   Doors, where my heart was used to beat
So quickly, waiting for a hand,

A hand that can be clasp'd no more –   5
   Behold me, for I cannot sleep,
   And like a guilty thing I creep
At earliest morning to the door.

He is not here; but far away
   The noise of life begins again,   10
   And ghastly thro' the drizzling rain
On the bald street breaks the blank day.

VIII–XXIII

*Tennyson struggles with grief and depression, his emotions
swinging between 'calm despair' and 'wild unrest'. The
thought that Hallam is being buried in England comforts
him, and he looks back on their friendship.*

XXIV

And was the day of my delight
   As pure and perfect as I say?
   The very source and fount of Day   15
Is dash'd with wandering isles of night.

If all was good and fair we met,
   This earth had been the Paradise
   It never look'd to human eyes
Since our first Sun arose and set.   20

And is it that the haze of grief
    Makes former gladness loom so great?
    The lowness of the present state,
That sets the past in this relief?

Or that the past will always win   25
    A glory from its being far;
    And orb° into the perfect star
We saw not, when we moved therein?

XXV

I know that this was Life, – the track
    Whereon with equal feet we fared;   30
    And then, as now, the day prepared
The daily burden for the back.

But this it was that made me move
    As light as carrier birds in air;
    I loved the weight I had to bear,   35
Because it needed help of Love.

Nor could I weary, heart or limb,
    When mighty Love would cleave° in twain
    The lading° of a single pain
And part it, giving half to him.   40

XXVI–XXVII

*Tennyson feels he must struggle with life alone, but is
consoled by his belief that "Tis better to have loved and lost
Than never to have loved at all'.*

The first Christmas

XXVIII

The time draws near the birth of Christ:
    The moon is hid; the night is still;
    The Christmas bells from hill to hill
Answer each other in the mist.

Four voices of four hamlets round,   45
    From far and near, on mead and moor,
    Swell out and fail, as if a door
Were shut between me and the sound:

Each voice four changes° on the wind,
    That now dilate, and now decrease,   50
    Peace and goodwill, goodwill and peace,
Peace and goodwill, to all mankind.

This year I slept and woke with pain,
    I almost wish'd no more to wake,
    And that my hold on life would break   55
Before I heard those bells again:

But they my troubled spirit rule,
    For they controll'd me when a boy;
    They bring me sorrow touch'd with joy,
The merry merry bells of Yule.°   60

XXIX

With such compelling cause to grieve
    As daily vexes household peace,
    And chains regret to his decease,
How dare we keep our Christmas-eve;

Which brings no more a welcome guest   65
    To enrich the threshold of the night
    With shower'd largess of delight
In dance and song and games and jest?

Yet go, and while the holly boughs
    Entwine the cold baptismal font,
    Make one wreath more for Use and Wont,   70
That guard the portals of the house;

Old sisters of a day gone by,
    Gray nurses, loving nothing new;
    Why should they miss their yearly due   75
Before their time? They too will die.

XXX

With trembling fingers did we weave
    The holly round the Christmas hearth;
    A rainy cloud possess'd the earth,
And sadly fell our Christmas-eve.   80

At our old pastimes in the hall
    We gambol'd, making vain pretence
    Of gladness, with an awful sense
Of one mute Shadow watching all.

We paused: the winds were in the beech: 85
    We heard them sweep the winter land;
    And in a circle hand-in-hand
Sat silent, looking each at each.

Then echo-like our voices rang;
    We sung, tho' every eye was dim,   90
    A merry song we sang with him
Last year: impetuously we sang:

We ceased: a gentler feeling crept
    Upon us: surely rest is meet:
    'They rest,' we said, 'their sleep is sweet,'   95
And silence follow'd, and we wept.

Our voices took a higher range;
    Once more we sang: 'They do not die
    Nor lose their mortal sympathy,
Nor change to us, although they change;   100

Rapt from the fickle and the frail
    With gather'd power, yet the same,
    Pierces the keen seraphic flame
From orb to orb, from veil to veil'.

Rise happy morn, rise, holy morn,   105
    Draw forth the cheerful day from night:
    O Father, touch the east, and light
The light that shone when hope was born.

XXXI–XLIX
*Tennyson comforts himself with the belief that Hallam's
spirit lives on after death.*

L
Be near me when my light is low,
    When the blood creeps, and the nerves prick   110
    And tingle; and the heart is sick,
And all the wheels of Being slow.

Be near me when the sensuous frame
    Is rack'd with pangs that conquer trust;
    And Time, a maniac scattering dust,   115
And Life, a Fury slinging flame.

Be near me when my faith is dry,
    And men the flies of latter spring,
    That lay their eggs, and sting and sing
And weave their petty cells and die.   120

Be near me when I fade away,
    To point the term of human strife,
    And on the low dark verge of life
The twilight of eternal day.

LI

Do we indeed desire the dead   125
    Should still be near us at our side?
    Is there no baseness we would hide?
No inner vileness that we dread?

Shall he for whose applause I strove,
    I had such reverence for his blame,   130
    See with clear eye some hidden shame
And I be lessen'd in his love?

I wrong the grave with fears untrue:
    Shall love be blamed for want of faith?
    There must be wisdom with great Death: 135
The dead shall look me thro' and thro'.

Be near us when we climb or fall:
    Ye watch, like God, the rolling hours
    With larger other eyes than ours,
To make allowance for us all.   140

LII–LXVI

Although shaken by religious doubts, Tennyson continues to
be comforted by belief in Hallam's spiritual guidance.

LXVII

When on my bed the moonlight falls,
    I know that in thy place of rest°
    By that broad water of the west,
There comes a glory on the walls:

Thy marble bright in dark appears,   145
    As slowly steals a silver flame
    Along the letters of thy name,
And o'er the number of thy years.

The mystic glory swims away;
    From off my bed the moonlight dies;   150
    And closing eaves of wearied eyes
I sleep till dusk is dipt in gray:

And then I know the mist is drawn
    A lucid veil from coast to coast,
    And in the dark church like a ghost   155
Thy tablet glimmers to the dawn.

LXVIII–LXXVII

Despite knowing that his poetry cannot do Hallam justice,
Tennyson must continue to write about his feelings.

The second Christmas

LXXVIII

Again at Christmas did we weave
    The holly round the Christmas hearth;
    The silent snow possess'd the earth,
And calmly fell our Christmas-eve: 160

The yule-clog sparkled keen with frost,
    No wing of wind the region swept,
    But over all things brooding slept
The quiet sense of something lost.

As in the winters left behind,   165
    Again our ancient games had place,
    The mimic picture's breathing grace,
And dance and song and hoodman-blind.⬥

Who show'd a token of distress?
    No single tear, no mark of pain: 170
    O sorrow, then can sorrow wane?
O grief, can grief be changed to less?

O last regret, regret can die!
    No – mixt with all this mystic frame,
    Her deep relations are the same,   175
But with long use her tears are dry.

LXXIX–CIV

*Tennyson begins to resolve his feelings about death and life,
love and loss, combining images of Spring and new growth
with a continual sense of spiritual communication with
Hallam.*

The third Christmas

CV

To-night ungather'd let us leave
    This laurel, let this holly stand:
    We live within the stranger's land,°
And strangely falls our Christmas-eve.   180

Our father's dust is left alone
    And silent under other snows:
    There in due time the woodbine blows,
The violet comes, but we are gone.

No more shall wayward grief abuse   185
    The genial hour with mask and mime;
    For change of place, like growth of time,
Has broke the bond of dying use.

Let cares that petty shadows cast,
    By which our lives are chiefly proved,   190
    A little spare the night I loved,
And hold it solemn to the past.

But let no footstep beat the floor,
    Nor bowl of wassail° mantle° warm;
    For who would keep an ancient form   195
Thro' which the spirit breathes no more?

Be neither song, nor game, nor feast;
    Nor harp be touch'd, nor flute be blown;
    No dance, no motion, save alone
What lightens in the lucid east   200

Of rising worlds by yonder wood.
    Long sleeps the summer in the seed;
    Run out your measured arcs, and lead
The closing cycle rich in good.

CVI

Ring out, wild bells, to the wild sky,   205
    The flying cloud, the frosty light:
    The year is dying in the night;
Ring out, wild bells, and let him die.

Ring out the old, ring in the new,
    Ring, happy bells, across the snow: 210
    The year is going, let him go;
Ring out the false, ring in the true.

Ring out the grief that saps the mind,
    For those that here we see no more;
    Ring out the feud of rich and poor,   215
Ring in redress to all mankind.

Ring out a slowly dying cause,
    And ancient forms of party strife;
    Ring in the nobler modes of life,
With sweeter manners, purer laws.   220

Ring out the want, the care, the sin,
    The faithless coldness of the times;
    Ring out, ring out thy mournful rhymes,
But ring the fuller minstrel in.

Ring out false pride in place and blood,   225
    The civic slander and the spite;
    Ring in the love of truth and right,
Ring in the common love of good.

Ring out old shapes of foul disease;
    Ring out the narrowing lust of gold;   230
    Ring out the thousand wars of old,
Ring in the thousand years of peace.

Ring in the valiant man and free,
    The larger heart, the kindlier hand;
    Ring out the darkness of the land,   235
Ring in the Christ that is to be.

CVII

It is the day when he was born,
    A bitter day that early sank
    Behind a purple-frosty bank
Of vapour, leaving night forlorn.   240

The time admits not flowers or leaves
    To deck the banquet. Fiercely flies
    The blast of North and East, and ice
Makes daggers at the sharpen'd eaves,

And bristles all the brakes and thorns   245
    To yon hard crescent, as she hangs
    Above the wood which grides° and clangs
Its leafless ribs and iron horns

Together, in the drifts that pass
    To darken on the rolling brine   250
    That breaks the coast. But fetch the wine,
Arrange the board and brim the glass;

Bring in great logs and let them lie,
    To make a solid core of heat;
    Be cheerful-minded, talk and treat   255
Of all things ev'n as he were by;

We keep the day. With festal cheer,
    With books and music, surely we
    Will drink to him, whate'er he be,
And sing the songs he loved to hear.   260

CVIII–CXIV

In Memoriam *ends hopefully. CXV is one of many lyrics that celebrates Tennyson's faith in human and spiritual love, strengthened by his grief and by his eventual coming to terms with Hallam's death.*

CXV

Now fades the last long streak of snow,
    Now burgeons every maze of quick°
    About the flowering squares, and thick
By ashen roots the violets blow.

Now rings the woodland loud and long,   265
    The distance takes a lovelier hue,
    And drown'd in yonder living blue
The lark becomes a sightless song.

Now dance the lights on lawn and lea,
    The flocks are whiter down the vale,   270
    And milkier every milky sail
On winding stream or distant sea;

Where now the seamew pipes, or dives
    In yonder greening gleam, and fly
    The happy birds, that change their sky   275
To build and brood; that live their lives

From land to land; and in my breast
    Spring wakens too; and my regret
    Becomes an April violet,
And buds and blossoms like the rest.   280

Maud (1855)

The plot of this long poem involves:

- a young man, whose dead father was ruined financially by Maud's father
- Maud's father, a rich lord
- Maud, a beautiful young woman
- Maud's brother, who hopes to become a Member of Parliament
- his rich friend, who wants to marry Maud.

✦ *Activity*

Before you read any of the extracts from the poem, use this list of characters, and your knowledge of dramatic romances, to invent your own story.

Maud: a Monodrama

A monodrama is a dramatic piece for one speaker. The term helps to distinguish *Maud* from Tennyson's other long poems. For example, his version of the Sleeping Beauty is a mixture of narrative and description, divided into several parts; *The Princess* is a 'medley' of lyrics and blank verse, and *In Memoriam* is a sequence of lyric poems on a theme. *Maud* is written in a number of sections and a variety of poetic forms, but from the point of view and in the voice of a single speaker.

This is Tennyson's own commentary on *Maud*, recorded by his son, Hallam Tennyson, in *Alfred, Lord Tennyson: a Memoir* in 1897:

> This poem is the history of a morbid, poetic soul,
> under the blighting influence of a recklessly
> speculative age. He is the heir of madness, an egoist
> with the makings of a cynic, raised to a pure and
> holy love which elevates his whole nature, passing
> from the height of triumph to the lowest depth of

misery, driven into madness by the loss of her whom he has loved, and when he has at length passed through the fiery furnace, and has recovered his reason, giving himself up to work for the good of mankind through the unselfishness born of a great passion. The peculiarity of this poem is that different phases of passion in one person take the place of different characters.

In your own story (see the Activity above), how important were the plot and events? Tennyson's original title for the poem was *Maud; or The Madness*, and you can see from his statement that what he is interested in is his speaker's different states of mind as the tragedy develops, not primarily in telling a story.

✦ *Activities*

1 Maud: a psychological case study

You have Tennyson's interpretation of the speaker's state of mind but as you study the poem, you may find that you disagree with him. This doesn't matter, provided that your own interpretation is based on a careful reading of the text.

Treat the extracts from Parts I and II as consultations with the patient, Mr X. What he says in each extract is the evidence on which you will produce your report of his case.

Your report will briefly refer to the events in X's life, but only in so far as these have a bearing on his state of mind. The main purpose of the report is to analyse the patient's moods and feelings, as revealed in what he says. Pay particular attention to:
- things he says about himself and others
- the feelings he expresses, about himself and others
- the tone and pace of his speech at different times
- the imagery he uses.

2 Finally, discuss the extract from Part III. This is how Tennyson ends the whole poem. What are your reactions to it as the conclusion of the poem if you read it:
- as the solution to X's problems
- as expressing Tennyson's attitude to 'the blighting influence of a recklessly speculative age' and his feelings about England in 1855, on the verge of the Crimean War?

from *Maud; A Monodrama*

Part I

I hate the dreadful hollow behind the little wood,
Its lips in the field above are dabbled with blood-red heath,
The red-ribb'd ledges drip with a silent horror of blood,
And Echo there, whatever is ask'd her, answers 'Death.'

For there in the ghastly pit long since a body was found,   5
His who had given me life – O father! O God! was it well? –
Mangled, and flatten'd, and crush'd, and dinted into the
      ground:
There yet lies the rock that fell with him when he fell.

Did he fling himself down? who knows? for a vast speculation
      had fail'd,
And ever he mutter'd and madden'd, and ever wann'd° with   10
      despair,
And out he walk'd when the wind like a broken worldling
      wail'd,
And the flying gold of the ruin'd woodlands drove thro' the air.

I remember the time, for the roots of my hair were stirr'd
By a shuffled step, by a dead weight trail'd, by a whisper'd
      fright,
And my pulses closed their gates with a shock on my heart as   15
      I heard
The shrill-edged shriek of a mother divide the shuddering night.

Villainy somewhere! whose? One says, we are villains all.
Not he: his honest fame should at least by me be maintained:
But that old man, now lord of the broad estate and the Hall,
Dropt off gorged from a scheme that had left us flaccid and   20
      drain'd.

Maud has returned home to the Hall. Although at first the
speaker thinks she is proud and unapproachable, he finds her
increasingly irresistible and reluctantly begins to fall in love.

Morning arises stormy and pale,
No sun, but a wannish glare
In fold upon fold of hueless cloud,
And the budded peaks of the wood are bow'd
Caught and cuff'd by the gale: 25
I had fancied it would be fair.

Whom but Maud should I meet
Last night, when the sunset burn'd
On the blossom'd gable-ends
At the head of the village street,   30
Whom but Maud should I meet?
And she touch'd my hand with a smile so sweet,
She made me divine amends
For a courtesy not return'd.

And thus a delicate spark   35
Of glowing and growing light
Thro' the livelong hours of the dark
Kept itself warm in the heart of my dreams,
Ready to burst in a colour'd flame;
Till at last when the morning came   40
In a cloud, it faded, and seems
But an ashen-gray delight.

What if with her sunny hair,
And smile as sunny as cold,
She meant to weave me a snare   45
Of some coquettish deceit,
Cleopatra-like as of old
To entangle me when we met,
To have her lion roll in a silken net
And fawn at a victor's feet.   50

Ah, what shall I be at fifty
Should Nature keep me alive,
If I find the world so bitter
When I am but twenty-five?
Yet, if she were not a cheat,   55
If Maud were all that she seem'd,
And her smile were all that I dream'd,
Then the world were not so bitter
But a smile could make it sweet.

What if tho' her eye seem'd full   60
Of a kind intent to me,
What if that dandy-despot, he,
That jewell'd mass of millinery,
That oil'd and curl'd Assyrian Bull
Smelling of musk[◇] and of insolence,   65
Her brother, from whom I keep aloof,
Who wants the finer politic sense
To mask, tho' but in his own behoof,[◇]
With a glassy smile his brutal scorn –
What if he had told her yestermorn   70
How prettily for his own sweet sake
A face of tenderness might be feign'd,
And a moist mirage in desert eyes,
That so, when the rotten hustings[◇] shake
In another month to his brazen lies,   75
A wretched vote may be gain'd.

For a raven ever croaks, at my side,
Keep watch and ward, keep watch and ward,
Or thou wilt prove their tool.
Yea, too, myself from myself I guard,   80
For often a man's own angry pride
Is cap and bells for a fool.

* * * * * *

Sick, am I sick of a jealous dread?
Was not one of the two at her side
This new-made lord, whose splendour plucks   85
The slavish hat from the villager's head?
Whose old grandfather has lately died,
Gone to a blacker pit, for whom
Grimy nakedness dragging his trucks
And laying his trams in a poison'd gloom   90
Wrought, till he crept from a gutted mine
Master of half a servile shire,
And left his coal all turn'd into gold
To a grandson, first of his noble line,
Rich in the grace all women desire,   95
Strong in the power that all men adore,
And simper and set their voices lower,
And soften as if to a girl, and hold
Awe-stricken breaths at a work divine,
Seeing his gewgaw⁰ castle shine,   100
New as his title, built last year,
There amid perky larches and pine,
And over the sullen-purple moor
(Look at it) pricking a cockney ear.

What, has he found my jewel out?   105
For one of the two that rode at her side
Bound for the Hall, I am sure was he:
Bound for the Hall, and I think for a bride,
Blithe would her brother's acceptance be.
Maud could be gracious too, no doubt   110
To a lord, a captain, a padded shape,
A bought commission, a waxen face,
A rabbit mouth that is ever agape –
Bought? what is it he cannot buy?
And therefore splenetic,⁰ personal, base,   115
A wounded thing with a rancorous cry,
At war with myself and a wretched race,
Sick, sick to the heart of life, am I.

68

Despite his doubts and possible obstacles put in their way by Maud's brother, his relationship with Maud develops. A ball, to which he is not invited, is held at the Hall. Passionately in love, he waits all night in the garden to speak to her. The next extract gives the first three and last three verses of the final section of Part I.

The Victorian language of flowers could be used to send messages to your beloved. It adds an extra layer of meaning to this lyric, as it does to some Victorian paintings:
lily = majesty, purity
rose = love
red rose = passion
white rose = I am not worthy of you
red and white roses together = unity

Come into the garden, Maud,
   For the black bat, night, has flown,   120
Come into the garden, Maud,
   I am here at the gate alone;
And the woodbine spices are wafted abroad,
   And the musk of the rose is blown.

For a breeze of morning moves,   125
   And the planet of Love is on high,
Beginning to faint in the light that she loves
   On a bed of daffodil sky,
To faint in the light of the sun she loves,
   To faint in his light, and to die.   130

All night have the roses heard
   The flute, violin, bassoon;
All night has the casement jessamine stirr'd
   To the dancers dancing in tune;
Till a silence fell with the waking bird,   135
   And a hush with the setting moon.

* * * * * *

Queen rose of the rosebud garden of girls,
    Come hither, the dances are done,
In gloss of satin and glimmer of pearls,
    Queen lily and rose in one;   140
Shine out, little head, sunning over with curls,
    To the flowers, and be their sun.

There has fallen a splendid tear
    From the passion-flower at the gate.
She is coming, my dove, my dear;   145
    She is coming, my life, my fate;
The red rose cries, 'She is near, she is near;'
    And the white rose weeps, 'She is late;'
The larkspur listens, 'I hear, I hear;'
    And the lily whispers, 'I wait.'   150

She is coming, my own, my sweet;
    Were it ever so airy a tread,
My heart would hear her and beat,
    Were it earth in an earthy bed;
My dust would hear her and beat,   155
    Had I lain for a century dead;
Would start and tremble under her feet,
    And blossom in purple and red.

Part II

'The fault was mine, the fault was mine' –
Why am I sitting here so stunn'd and still,   160
Plucking the harmless wild-flower on the hill? –
It is this guilty hand! –
And there rises ever a passionate cry
From underneath in the darkening land –
What is it, that has been done?   165
O dawn of Eden bright over earth and sky,
The fires of Hell brake out of thy rising sun,
The fires of Hell and of Hate;
For she, sweet soul, had hardly spoken a word,
When her brother ran in his rage to the gate,   170
He came with the babe-faced lord;
Heap'd on her terms of disgrace,
And while she wept, and I strove to be cool,
He fiercely gave me the lie,
Till I with as fierce an anger spoke,   175
And he struck me, madman, over the face,
Struck me before the languid fool,
Who was gaping and grinning by:
Struck for himself an evil stroke;
Wrought for his house an irredeemable woe;   180
For front to front in an hour we stood,
And a million horrible bellowing echoes broke
From the red-ribb'd hollow behind the wood,
And thunder'd up into Heaven the Christ-less code,
That must have life for a blow.   185
Ever and ever afresh they seem'd to grow.
Was it he lay there with a fading eye?
'The fault was mine,' he whisper'd, 'fly!'
Then glided out of the joyous wood
The ghastly Wraith of one that I know;   190
And there rang on a sudden a passionate cry,
A cry for a brother's blood:
It will ring in my heart and my ears, till I die, till I die.

Having accidentally killed Maud's brother in a duel, he escapes abroad, where he hears that Maud has also died. He returns to England, haunted by memories of her. The next extract is the beginning and end of the final section of Part II.

Dead, long dead,
Long dead!   195
And my heart is a handful of dust,
And the wheels go over my head,
And my bones are shaken with pain,
For into a shallow grave they are thrust,
Only a yard beneath the street,   200
And the hoofs of the horses beat, beat,
The hoofs of the horses beat,
Beat into my scalp and my brain,
With never an end to the stream of passing feet,
Driving, hurrying, marrying, burying,   205
Clamour and rumble, and ringing and clatter,
And here beneath it is all as bad,
For I thought the dead had peace, but it is not so;
To have no peace in the grave, is that not sad?
But up and down and to and fro,   210
Ever about me the dead men go;
And then to hear a dead man chatter
Is enough to drive one mad.

* * * * * *

O me, why have they not buried me deep enough?
Is it kind to have made me a grave so rough,   215
Me, that was never a quiet sleeper?
Maybe still I am but half-dead;
Then I cannot be wholly dumb;
I will cry to the steps above my head
And somebody, surely, some kind heart will come   220
To bury me, bury me
Deeper, ever so little deeper.

Part III

After many months of madness and horror, the speaker at
last begins to recover. He is helped by a dream in which
Maud urges him to fight for his country in the war which is
about to break out.

And as months ran on and rumour of battle grew,
'It is time, it is time, O passionate heart,' said I
(For I cleaved to a cause that I felt to be pure and true),   225
'It is time, O passionate heart and morbid eye,
That old hysterical mock disease should die.'
And I stood on a giant deck and mix'd my breath
With a loyal people shouting a battle cry,
Till I saw the dreary phantom arise and fly   230
Far into the North, and battle, and seas of death.

Let it go or stay, so I wake to the higher aims
Of a land that has lost for a little her lust of gold,
And love of a peace that was full of wrongs and shames,
Horrible, hateful, monstrous, not to be told;   235
And hail once more to the banner of battle unroll'd!
                              * * * * * *
For the peace, that I deem'd no peace, is over and done,
And now by the side of the Black and the Baltic deep,◇
And deathful-grinning mouths of the fortress, flames
The blood-red blossom of war with a heart of fire.   240

Let it flame or fade, and the war roll down like a wind,
We have proved we have hearts in a cause, we are noble still,
And myself have awaked, as it seems, to the better mind;
It is better to fight for the good than to rail at the ill;
I have felt with my native land, I am one with my kind,   245
I embrace the purpose of God, and the doom assign'd.

Crossing the Bar (1889)

Tennyson said of this poem, which he wrote three years before his death: 'Mind you put my "Crossing the Bar" at the end of all editions of my poems.' What can you find in this poem which makes it an appropriate conclusion to his work?

Crossing the Bar

Sunset and evening star,
    And one clear call for me!
And may there be no moaning of the bar,◇
    When I put out to sea,

But such a tide as moving seems asleep,   5
    Too full for sound and foam,
When that which drew from out the boundless deep
    Turns again home.

Twilight and evening bell,
    And after that the dark!   10
And may there be no sadness of farewell,
    When I embark;

For tho' from out our bourne of Time and Place
    The flood may bear me far,
I hope to see my Pilot face to face   15
    When I have crost the bar.

Elizabeth Barrett Browning
(1806–1861)

Elizabeth Barrett Browning's poetry was very popular while she was alive, but since her death most readers have been more interested in the romantic details of her life before and after her marriage to Robert Browning. In her work she wanted to write truthfully about contemporary subjects. She tackled political and social issues, as well as writing personal poems and a 'verse-novel' in which she explored aspects of the oppression of women in the nineteenth century, and their difficulties in achieving independence.

The Cry of the Children (1843)

The Greek quotation from Euripides' play, *Medea*, at the beginning of the poem means:

> Woe, woe, why do you look upon me with your
> eyes, my children?

In the play, Medea, the woman who helped Jason steal the Golden Fleece and was betrayed by him, says this just before she murders her own children.

In 1842 and 1843 Parliamentary Reports were published by the Commissioners on the *Employment of Children and Young Persons in Mines and Manufacturies*. Here are some of their findings.

> We find:

> That instances occur in which children are taken into these mines to work as early as four years of age, sometimes at five, and between five and six, and often from seven to eight, while from eight to nine is the ordinary age at which employment in these mines commences.

That the regular hours of work for Children and Young Persons are rarely less than eleven; more often they are twelve; in some districts thirteen; in one district they are fourteen and upwards.

That ... some of the Children are robust, active and healthy, although in general even these are undersized; but that from the early ages at which the great majority commence work, from the long hours of work, and from the insufficiency of their food and clothing, their 'bodily health' is seriously and generally injured; they are for the most part stunted in growth, their aspect being pale, delicate and sickly, and they present altogether the appearance of a race which has suffered general physical deterioration.

(*Children's Employment Commission (Mines); Parliamentary Papers*, 1842)

'The Cry of the Children' was first published in *Blackwood's Edinburgh Magazine* in 1843, and contributed to changes being made in the laws governing the employment of children.

✦ *Activity*

The Parliamentary report states facts; Elizabeth Barrett Browning is writing to shock, to move and to persuade. How does she do this? Why do you think she put the quotation from Euripides at the beginning of her poem?

a   Discuss the techniques she uses in her poem which you might also find in a political speech. Look at the ways she uses:
  • rhetorical questions
  • contrasts
  • quotations
  • exclamations
  • repetitions.

b   Is it a speech, or is it a poem? In small groups prepare alternative presentations of some selected verses from 'The Cry of the Children'. Aim to help your audience to hear the poem as poetry, as well as political oratory.

The Cry of the Children

'φεν, φεν, τι προσδερκεσθε μ ομμασιυ, τεκυα.' Medea

Do ye hear the children weeping, O my brothers,
    Ere the sorrow comes with years?
They are leaning their young heads against their mothers, –
    And *that* cannot stop their tears.
The young lambs are bleating in the meadows;   5
    The young birds are chirping in the nest;
The young fawns are playing with the shadows;
    The young flowers are blowing toward the west –
But the young, young children, O my brothers,
    They are weeping bitterly! –   10
They are weeping in the playtime of the others,
    In the country of the free.

Do you question the young children in the sorrow,
    Why their tears are falling so? –
The old man may weep for his to-morrow   15
    Which is lost in Long Ago –
The old tree is leafless in the forest –
    The old year is ending in the frost –
The old wound, if stricken, is the sorest –
    The old hope is hardest to be lost: 20
But the young, young children, O my brothers,
    Do you ask them why they stand
Weeping sore before the bosoms of their mothers,
    In our happy Fatherland?

They look up with their pale and sunken faces,   25
    And their looks are sad to see,
For the man's grief abhorrent, draws and presses
    Down the cheeks of infancy –
'Your old earth,' they say, 'is very dreary;'
    'Our young feet,' they say, 'are very weak!   30

Few paces have we taken, yet are weary –
    Our grave-rest is very far to seek.
Ask the old why they weep, and not the children,
       For the outside earth is cold, –
And we young ones stand without, in our bewildering,   35
       And the graves are for the old.

'True,' say the young children, 'it may happen
    That we die before our time!
Little Alice died last year – the grave is shapen
       Like a snowball, in the rime.   40
We looked into the pit prepared to take her –
    Was no room for any work in the close clay:
From the sleep wherein she lieth none will wake her,
    Crying, "Get up, little Alice! it is day".
If you listen by that grave, in sun and shower,   45
    With your ear down, little Alice never cries! –
Could we see her face, be sure we should not know her,
    For the smile has time for growing in her eyes, –
And merry go her moments, lulled and stilled in
    The shroud, by the kirk-chime!⋄   50
It is good when it happens,' say the children,
    'That we die before our time.'

Alas, the wretched children! they are seeking
    Death in life, as best to have!
They are binding up their hearts away from breaking,   55
    With a cerement⋄ from the grave.
Go out, children, from the mine and from the city –
    Sing out, children, as the little thrushes do –
Pluck your handfuls of the meadow-cowslips pretty –
    Laugh aloud, to feel your fingers let them through!   60
But they answer, 'Are your cowslips of the meadows
    Like our weeds anear the mine?
Leave us quiet in the dark of the coal-shadows,
    From your pleasures fair and fine!

'For oh,' say the children, 'we are weary,   65
    And we cannot run or leap –
If we cared for any meadows, it were merely
    To drop down in them and sleep.
Our knees tremble sorely in the stooping –
    We fall upon our faces, trying to go;   70
And, underneath our heavy eyelids drooping,
    The reddest flower would look as pale as snow.
For, all day, we drag our burden tiring,
    Through the coal-dark, underground –
Or, all day, we drive the wheels of iron   75
    In the factories, round and round.

'For, all day, the wheels are droning, turning, –
    Their wind comes in our faces, –
Till our hearts turn, – our head, with pulses burning,
    And the walls turn in their places –   80
Turns the sky in the high window blank and reeling –
    Turns the long light that droppeth down the wall –
Turn the black flies that crawl along the ceiling –
    All are turning, all the day, and we with all! –
And all day, the iron wheels are droning;   85
    And sometimes we could pray,
"O ye wheels," (breaking out in a mad moaning)
    "Stop! be silent for to-day!" '

Ay, be silent! Let them hear each other breathing
    For a moment, mouth to mouth –   90
Let them touch each other's hands, in a fresh wreathing
    Of their tender human youth!
Let them feel that this cold metallic motion
    Is not all the life God fashions or reveals –
Let them prove their inward souls against the notion   95
    That they live in you, or under you, O wheels! –
Still, all day, the iron wheels go onward,
    As if Fate in each were stark;
And the children's souls, which God is calling sunward,
    Spin on blindly in the dark.   100

Now tell the poor young children, O my brothers,
    That they look to Him and pray –
So the blessed One, who blesseth all the others,
    Will bless them another day.
They answer, 'Who is God that He should hear us,   105
    While the rushing of the iron wheels is stirred?
When we sob aloud, the human creatures near us
    Pass by, hearing not, or answer not a word!
And *we* hear not (for the wheels in their resounding)
    Strangers speaking at the door: 110
Is it likely God, with angels singing round Him,
    Hears our weeping any more?

'Two words, indeed, of praying we remember;
    And at midnight's hour of harm, –
"Our Father," looking upward in the chamber,   115
    We say softly for a charm.
We know no other words, except "Our Father,"
    And we think that, in some pause of angels' song,
God may pluck them with the silence sweet to gather,
    And hold both within His right hand which is strong.   120
"Our Father!" If He heard us, He would surely
    (For they call Him good and mild)
Answer, smiling down the steep world very purely,
    "Come and rest with me, my child."'

'But, no!' say the children, weeping faster,   125
    'He is speechless as a stone;
And they tell us, of His image is the master
    Who commands us to work on.
Go to!' say the children, – 'Up in Heaven,
    Dark, wheel-like, turning clouds are all we find.   130
Do not mock us; grief has made us unbelieving –
    We look up for God, but tears have made us blind.'
Do you hear the children weeping and disproving,
    O my brothers, what ye preach?
For God's possible is taught by His world's loving –   135
    And the children doubt of each.

And well may the children weep before you;
    They are weary ere they run;
They have never seen the sunshine, nor the glory
    Which is brighter than the sun: 140
They know the grief of man, but not the wisdom;
    They sink in the despair, without the calm –
Are slaves, without the liberty in Christdom, –
    Are martyrs, by the pang without the palm, –
Are worn, as if with age, yet unretrievingly   145
    No dear remembrance keep, –
Are orphans of the earthly love and heavenly:
    Let them weep! let them weep!

They look up, with their pale and sunken faces,
    And their look is dread to see,   150
For you think you see their angels in their places,
    With eyes meant for Deity; –
'How long,' they say, 'how long, O cruel nation,
    Will you stand, to move the world, on a child's heart, –
Stifle down with a mailed heel its palpitation,   155
    And tread onward to your throne amid the mart?◇
Our blood splashes upward, O our tyrants,
    And your purple shows your path;
But the child's sob curseth deeper in the silence
    Than the strong man in his wrath!'   160

The Runaway Slave at Pilgrim's Point (1848)

Elizabeth Barrett Browning's family owned and managed sugar plantations in Jamaica. This poem was written for anti-slavery protesters in America, and first published in Boston in 1848, as the 'Advertisement' at the beginning explains. In 1848, Elizabeth Barrett Browning had escaped to Italy with Robert Browning. It is one of the first poems which she wrote after she had run away from her life as an invalid and escaped from her father's control; she was herself pregnant when she wrote the poem.

✦ *Activities*

1 The poem is written from the point of view of a runaway slave. With a partner, talk about how much you have learned about the speaker's life from the poem. How successfully has Elizabeth Barrett Browning managed to convey the slave's experiences and feelings to you? Do you think there might be any links between the poem and the poet's own life at the time she was writing it?

2 Having read 'The Cry of the Children' and 'The Runaway Slave', do you think that poetry is an effective medium for messages like these? If so, why? If not, why not?

The Runaway Slave at Pilgrim's Point

[ADVERTISEMENT, The following verses were the contribution of the Authoress to a volume entitled 'The Liberty Bell, by Friends of Freedom,' printed in America last year for sale at the Boston National Anti-Slavery Bazaar. It is for the use of a few 'friends of freedom' and of the writer on this side of the Atlantic that the verses are now reprinted. FLORENCE, 1849.]

I

I stand on the mark, beside the shore
   Of the first white pilgrim's bended knee,
Where exile changed to ancestor,
   And God was thanked for liberty.
I have run through the night – my skin is as dark –   5
I bend my knee down on this mark: –
   I look on the sky and the sea.

II

O, pilgrim-souls, I speak to you:
   I see you come out proud and slow
From the land of the spirits, pale as dew,   10
   And round me and round me ye go.
O pilgrims, I have gasped and run
All night long from the whips of one
   Who, in your names, works sin and woe.

III

At the place where the pilgrims landed years before in search of freedom, the slave curses America.

IV

I am black – I am black!   15
   And yet God made me, they say:
But *if* He did so, smiling, back
   He must have cast His work away
Under the feet of His white creatures,
With a look of scorn, that the dusky features   20
   Might be trodden again to clay.

V

And yet He has made dark things
   To be glad and merry as light:
There's a little dark bird sits and sings;
   There's a dark stream ripples out of sight;   25
And the dark frogs chant in the safe morass,
And the sweetest stars are made to pass
   O'er the face of the darkest night.

VI

But *we* who are dark, we are dark!
   O God, we have no stars!   30
About our souls, in care and cark,◇
   Our blackness shuts like prison bars:
And crouch our souls so far behind,
That never a comfort can they find
   By reaching through the prison-bars.   35

VII–VIII

*To Nature, there is no difference between a black person and
a white one.*

IX

I am black, I am black!
    And, once, I laughed in girlish glee;
For one of my colour stood in the track
    Where the drivers drove, and looked at me –
And tender and full was the look he gave!   40
A Slave looked *so* at another Slave, –
    I look at the sky and the sea.

X

And from that hour our spirits grew
    As free as if unsold, unbought:
We were strong enough, since we were two,   45
    To conquer the world, we thought!
The drivers drove us day by day;
We did not mind, we went one way
    And no better a liberty sought.

XI–XIII

*She describes a happy, loving relationship, which the slave
owners destroy.*

XIV

We were black, we were black!   50
    We had no claim to love and bliss;
What marvel, ours was cast to wrack?
    They wrung my cold hands out of his, –
They dragged him – where? I crawled to touch
His blood's mark in the dust – not much,   55
    Ye pilgrim-souls, – though plain as *this!*

XV

Wrong, followed by a greater wrong!
   Grief seemed too good for such as I:
So the white men brought the shame ere long
   To stifle the sob in my throat thereby.   60
They would not leave me for my dull
Wet eyes! – it was too merciful
   To let me weep pure tears, and die.

XVI

I am black, I am black!
   I wore a child upon my breast –   65
An amulet° that hung too slack,
   And, in my unrest, could not rest:
Thus we went moaning, child and mother,
One to another, one to another,
   Until all ended for the best.   70

XVII

For hark! I will tell you low – low –
   I am black, you see, –
And the babe, who lay on my bosom so,
   Was far too white, too white for me;
As white as the ladies who scorned to pray   75
Beside me at church but yesterday,
   Though my tears had washed a place for my knee.

XVIII

And my own child! I could not bear
   To look in his face, it was so white;
I covered him up with a kerchief rare,   80
   I covered his face in, close and tight:
And he moaned and struggled, as well might be,
For the white child wanted his liberty –
   Ha, ha! he wanted the master's right.

XIX

He moaned and beat with his head and feet,   85
   His little feet that never grew;
He struck them out, as it was meet,
   Against my heart to break it through.
I might have sung like a mother –
But I dared not sing to the white-faced child   90
   The only song I knew.

XX

And yet I pulled the kerchief close:
   He could not see the sun, I swear
More, then, alive, than now he does
   From beneath the roots of the mango – where?   95
I know where. Close! A child and mother
Do wrong to look at one another,
   When one is black and the other is fair.

XXI

Even in that single glance I had
   Of my child's face, – I tell you all, –   100
I saw a look that made me mad! –
   The *master's* look, that used to fall
On my soul like his lash ... or worse! –
Therefore, to save it from my curse
   I twisted it round in my shawl.   105

XXII

And he moaned and trembled from foot to head,
   He shivered from head to foot, –
Till, after a time, he lay, instead,
   Too suddenly still and mute.
And I felt, beside, a creeping cold –   110
I dared to lift up just a fold,
   As in lifting a leaf of the mango-fruit.

* * * * * *

XXV

From the white man's house, and the black man's hut,
    I carried the little body on;
The forest's arms did round us shut,   115
    And silence through the trees did run!
They asked no questions as I went, –
They stood too high for astonishment, –
    They could see God rise on his throne.

XXVI

My little body, kerchiefed fast,   120
    I bore it on through the forest – on –
And when I felt it was tired at last,
    I scooped a hole beneath the moon.
Through the forest-tops the angels far,
With a white fine finger in every star,   125
    Did point and mock at what was done.

XXVII

Yet when it was all done aright,
    Earth, 'twixt me and my baby strewed, –
All changed to black earth, – nothing white, –
    A dark child in the dark, – ensued   130
Some comfort, and my heart grew young;
I sate down smiling there, and sung
    The song I told you of, for good.

XXVIII

And thus we two were reconciled,
    The white child and black mother, thus;   135
For, as I sang it, – soft, slow and wild
    The same song, more melodious,
Rose from the grave whereon I sate!
It was the dead child singing that,
    To join the souls of both of us.   140

XXIX–XXXI

*She realises she is surrounded by white men who have come
to capture her.*

XXXII

I am not mad: I am black!
   I see you staring in my face –
I know you staring, shrinking back! …
   Ye are born of the Washington race:
And this land is the Free America –   145
And this mark on my wrist, (I prove what I say)
   Ropes tied me up here to the flogging-place.

XXXIII

You think I shrieked then? Not a sound!
   I hung as a gourd hangs in the sun:
I only cursed them all around,   150
   As softly as I might have done
My own child after. From these sands
Up to the mountains, lift your hands,
   O Slaves, and end what I began!

XXXIV

Whips, curses; these must answer those!   155
   For in this UNION,° you have set
Two kinds of men in adverse rows,
   Each loathing each! and all forget
The seven wounds in Christ's body fair;
While HE see gaping everywhere   160
   Our countless wounds that pay no debt.

XXXV

Our wounds are different. Your white men
   Are, after all, not gods indeed,
Nor able to make Christ's again
   Do good with bleeding. *We* who bleed –   165
(Stand off) – *we* help not in our loss, –
We are too heavy for our cross,
   And fall and crush you and your seed.

XXXVI

I fall, I swoon!⁺ I look at the sky.
    The clouds are breaking on my brain;   170
I am floated along, as if I should die
    Of Liberty's exquisite pain –
In the name of the white child waiting for me
In the deep black death where our kisses agree, –
White men, I leave you all curse-free   175
    In my broken heart's disdain!

Sonnets from the Portuguese (1846)

During their courtship, as well as exchanging many letters, sometimes several in a day, Elizabeth Barrett Browning wrote a sequence of forty-four sonnets which describe her emotions and love for Robert Browning. Because she had heard him making uncomplimentary remarks about 'personal poetry' she kept the sonnets secret until after the birth of their son, Pen, in 1849. Browning, pleased and flattered by the gift, urged her to publish them, and suggested the title *Sonnets from the Portuguese*, partly to disguise their personal nature, and partly as an allusion to an earlier poem of hers, 'Caterina to Camões' in which the dying Caterina expresses her love for the great Portuguese poet, Camões.

In Sonnet XLIV Elizabeth Barrett Browning uses the language of flowers, and the symbolic meanings attached to them, as Tennyson does in 'Come into the garden, Maud':

rue – bitterness
eglantine (honeysuckle) – poetry
ivy – faithfulness

✦ *Activities*

1 What are your reactions to these love poems? If you were in love with someone, which one would you choose to give to them?

2 With a partner, or in a small group, discuss how Elizabeth Barrett Browning presents herself and her relationship with Robert Browning in these sonnets. (Remember that when she wrote them she was nearly forty years old, she had been an invalid for some time, and often felt too ill to leave her room.)

3 These sonnets have been printed with the original punctuation. Choose one, and discuss with a partner how you would punctuate it more conventionally. What effect does Elizabeth Barrett Browning's punctuation have on the way you read her poem?

Sonnets from the Portuguese

VI

Go from me. Yet I feel that I shall stand
Henceforward in thy shadow nevermore
Alone upon the threshold of my door
Of individual life, I shall command
The uses of my soul, nor lift my hand   5
Serenely in the sunshine as before,
Without the sense of that which I forbore, …
Thy touch upon the palm – The widest land
Doom takes to part us, leaves thy heart in mine
With pulses that beat double. What I do   10
And what I dream include thee, as the wine
Must taste of its own grapes. And when I sue
God for myself, He hears that name of thine,
And sees within my eyes, the tears of two –

VIII

What can I give thee back, o liberal   15
And princely giver, … who hast brought the gold
And purple of thine heart, unstained … untold …
And laid them on the outside of the wall
For such as I to take or leave withal,
In unexpected largesse? Am I cold,   20
Ungrateful … that for these most manifold
High gifts, I render nothing back at all?
Not so – not cold! – but very poor instead! –
Ask God who knows! – for frequent tears have run
The colours from my life, and left so dead   25
And pale a stuff, it were not fitly done
To give the same as pillow to thy head –
Go farther! – Let it serve to trample on –

X

Yet, love, mere love, is beautiful indeed
And worthy of acceptation. Fire is bright,   30
Let temple burn, or flax! – an equal light
Leaps in the flame from cedar-plank or weed –
And love is fire! – and when I say at need
I *love thee* ... mark! ... *I love thee!* ... in thy sight
I stand transfigured, glorified aright   35
With conscience of the new rays that proceed
Out of my face to thine. There's nothing low
In love, when love the lowest, – meanest creatures
Who love God, God accepts while loving so –
And what I *feel*, across the inferior features   40
Of what I *am*, doth flash itself, and show
How that great work of Love enhances Nature's.

XIV

If thou must love me, let it be for nought
Except for love's sake only. Do not say
'I love her for her smile ... her look ... her way   45
Of speaking gently ... ; for a trick of thought
That falls in well with mine, and certes brought
A sense of pleasant ease on such a day – '
For these things in themselves, beloved, may
Be changed, or change for thee, ... and love so wrought,   50
May be unwrought so. Neither love me for
Thine own dear pity wiping my cheeks dry! –
For one might well forget to weep, who bore
Thy comfort long, and lose thy love thereby –
But love me for love's sake, that evermore   55
Thou may'st love on through love's eternity –

XXVII

My own belovd, who hast lifted me
From this drear flat of earth where I was thrown, –
And in betwixt the languid ringlets blown
A life-breath, till the forehead hopefully   60
Shines out again as all the angels see,

94

Against thy saving kiss! ... My own, my own ...
Who camest to me when the world was gone,
And I who looked for only God, found *thee!*
I find thee! – I am safe, & strong, & glad! –   65
As one who stands in dewless asphodel°
Looks backward on the tedious time he had
In the upper life ... so I, with bosom = swell,
Make witness here between the good & bad,
That Love, as strong as Death, retrieves as well.   70

XXVIII

My letters! – all dead paper, ... mute and white! –
And yet they seem alive and quivering
Against my tremulous hands which loose the string
And let them drop down on my knee tonight.
This said, ... he wished to have me in his sight   75
Once, as a friend = this fixed a day in spring
To come and touch my hand ... a simple thing, ...
Yet I wept for it! – This ... the paper's light ...
Said, *Dear, I love thee!* – and I sank & quailed
As if God's future thundered on my past =   80
This said, '*I am thine*' – and so, its ink has paled
With lying at my heart that beats too fast =
And this ... O love, thy words have ill availed,
If, what this said, I dared repeat at last! –

XXXVIII

First time he kissed me, he but only kissed   85
The fingers of this hand wherewith I write,
And ever since it grew more clean and white ...
Slow to world-greetings ... quick with its 'oh, list'
When the angels speake. A ring of amethyst,
I could not wear here plainer to my sight,   90
Than that first kiss! – The second passed in height
The first, & sought the forehead, & half missed,
Half falling on the hair ... O beyond meed!° –
That was the chrism° of Love, which Love's own crown,
With sanctifying sweetness, did precede! –   95

The third, upon my lips, – was folded down
In perfect, purple state! – since when, indeed,
I have been proud and said, 'My Love, my own'.

XLIII

How do I love thee? Let me count the ways! –
I love thee to the depth & breadth & height   100
My soul can reach, when feeling out of sight
For the ends of Being and Ideal Grace.
I love thee to the level of everyday's
Most quiet need, by sun & candlelight –
I love thee freely, as men strive for Right, –   105
I love thee purely, as they turn from Praise;
I love thee with the passion, put to use
In my old griefs, … and with my childhood's faith:
I love thee with the love I seemed to lose
With my lost Saints, – I love thee with the breath,   110
Smiles, tears, of all my life! – and, if God choose,
I shall but love thee better after my death.

XLIV

Beloved, thou hast brought me many flowers
Plucked in the garden all the summer through,
And winter, and it seemed as if they grew   115
In this close room, nor missed the sun & showers.
So, in the like name of that love of ours,
Take back these thoughts, which here, unfolded, too,
And which on warm & cold days I withdrew
From my heart's ground. (Indeed, those beds and bowers   120
Be overgrown with bitter weeds & rue,
And wait thy weeding; yet here's eglantine,
Here's ivy!) – take them, as I used to do
Thy flowers, and keep them where they shall not pine!
Instruct thine eyes to keep their colours true,   125
And tell thy soul, their roots are left in mine.

Aurora Leigh (1856)

Aurora Leigh is the name of the heroine of a 'sort of novel-poem', as Elizabeth Barrett Browning described it herself. In a letter to Robert Browning before they were married she told him she was planning a:

> completely modern poem ... running into the midst
> of our conventions and rushing into drawing rooms
> and the like, 'where angels fear to tread'; and so,
> meeting face to face and without mask the
> Humanity of the age, and speaking the truth as I
> conceive of it plainly. That is my intention.

Aurora Leigh is written in nine books. As well as telling the story of Aurora's struggle to earn her own living as an independent woman by her writing, the poem contains social comment and criticism, elements of Elizabeth Barrett Browning's own life story and her views on art and literature. It was first published in 1856, and was enormously popular with her contemporaries.

Extract from Book 1

Aurora's father dies. Now an orphan, she is sent from Italy to England to be brought up by her aunt. In this extract Aurora describes her education.

✦ *Activity*

With a partner, work out the aunt's idea of a suitable curriculum for a thirteen-year-old girl, and her reasons for educating Aurora as she does. Role play a conversation between Aurora and her aunt, in which Aurora tries to persuade her aunt to let her stop learning some of the subjects she likes least.

Extract from Book 2

On her twentieth birthday, Aurora's cousin, Romney Leigh, proposes to her. He wants her to marry him so that she can help him with his plan for setting up a community, run on socialist principles. Aurora, who intends to earn her living by writing poetry, refuses him, saying:

> 'Why, sir, you are married long ago.
> You have a wife already whom you love,
> Your social theory.'

The extract continues her reply.

✦ *Activities*

1 Tennyson's Princess (see page 42) accepts the prince's proposal; Aurora rejects Romney's (although at the end of the 'novel-poem' she does eventually accept him). Basing what you say on the extracts from the poems, role play, or write, a dialogue between the Princess and Aurora, in which they discuss their decisions and each tries to persuade the other to change her mind.

2 The speech from *The Princess* (see page 45) is written for a male speaker by a man; the extracts from *Aurora Leigh* are written for a woman speaker by a woman. What can you deduce from them about Victorian attitudes to women and their relationships with men?

Extract from Book 5

In this extract, Elizabeth Barrett Browning uses Aurora to express her views about the role of the poet and the subject matter she thinks poetry should deal with. She argues strongly that poets should write about life and contemporary subjects, rather than 'poetic', picturesque ones set in a romantic, imaginary past.

In the remainder of *Aurora Leigh*, Aurora maintains her independence, and survives on her writing. She meets a poor girl, Marion Erle, and learns her life story, which is one of terrible poverty and degradation. She supports Marion and her child, and eventually accepts Romney's second proposal, after he (like Mr Rochester in *Jane Eyre*) has lost his sight in a fire.

✦ *Activities*

1 What impressions of Aurora's character do you get from these three extracts? Imagine you are either her aunt, or Romney, or a fellow writer, writing a letter to a close friend. Describe Aurora to them, making clear what strikes you most about her personality, and how you react to her.

2 Elizabeth Barrett Browning respected Tennyson as a poet, but disapproved of writers like him who seemed more often inspired by the Middle Ages, and stories of knights and maidens, than by their own times.

   a Imagine you are Elizabeth Barrett Browning and write a review of one of Tennyson's 'medieval' poems (on pages 16 to 36), trying to balance what you admire about it with what you dislike.

   b With a partner, improvise or script a discussion about writing poetry between Tennyson and Elizabeth Barrett Browning.

Aurora Leigh

from Book 1

                                   So it was.
I broke the copious curls upon my head
In braids, because she liked smooth-ordered hair.
I left off saying my sweet Tuscan words
Which still at any stirring of the heart   5
Came up to float across the English phrase
As lilies, (*Bene* … or *che ch'è*)◇ because
She liked my father's child to speak his tongue.
I learnt the collects and the catechism,
The creeds, from Athanasius back to Nice,   10
The Articles … the Tracts *against* the times,
(By no means Buonaventure's 'Prick of Love,')
And various popular synopses of
Inhuman doctrines never taught by John,
Because she liked instructed piety.◇   15
I learnt my complement of classic French
(Kept pure of Balzac◇ and neologism,◇)
And German also, since she liked a range
Of liberal education, – tongues, not books.
I learnt a little algebra, a little   20
Of the mathematics, – brushed with extreme flounce
The circle of the sciences, because
She misliked women who are frivolous.
I learnt the royal genealogies
Of Oviedo,◇ the internal laws   25
Of the Burmese empire, … by how many feet
Mount Chimborazo◇ outsoars Himmeleh.
What navigable river joins itself
To Lara, and what census of the year five
Was taken at Klagenfurt, – because she liked   30
A general insight into useful facts.
I learnt much music, – such as would have been
As quite impossible in Johnson's day

As still it might be wished – fine sleights of hand
And unimagined fingering, shuffling off   35
The hearer's soul through hurricanes of notes
To a noisy Tophet;◇ and I drew … costumes
From French engravings, nereids neatly draped
With smirks of simmering godship, – I washed in
From nature, landscapes, (rather say, washed out.)   40
I danced the polka and Cellarius,◇
Spun glass, stuffed birds, and modelled flowers in wax,
Because she liked accomplishment in girls.
I read a score of books on womanhood
To prove, if women do not think at all,   45
They may teach thinking, (to a maiden aunt
Or else the author) – books demonstrating
Their right of comprehending husband's talk
When not too deep, and even of answering
With pretty 'may it please you,' or 'so it is,' –   50
Their rapid insight and fine aptitude,
Particular worth and general missionariness,
As long as they keep quiet by the fire
And never say 'no' when the world says 'ay,'
For that is fatal, – their angelic reach   55
Of virtue, chiefly used to sit and darn,
And fatten household sinners, – their, in brief,
Potential faculty in everything
Of abdicating power in it:

from Book 2

With quiet indignation I broke in.   60
'You misconceive the question like a man,
Who sees a woman as the complement
Of his sex merely. You forget too much
That every creature, female as the male,
Stands single in responsible act and thought,   65
As also in birth and death. Whoever says
To a loyal woman, "Love and work with me,"
Will get fair answers, if the work and love,
Being good themselves, are good for her – the best

She was born for. Woman of a softer mood, 70
Surprised by men when scarcely awake to life,
Will sometimes only hear the first word, love,
And catch up with it any kind of work,
Indifferent, so that dear love go with it:
I do not blame such women, though, for love, 75
They pick much oakum;⋄ earth's fanatics make
Too frequently heaven's saints. But *me*, your work
Is not the best for, – nor your love the best,
Nor able to commend the kind of work
For love's sake merely. Ah, you force me, sir, 80
To be over-bold in speaking of myself, –
I, too, have my vocation, – work to do.

from Book 5
But poets should
Exert a double vision; should have eyes
To see near things as comprehensively
As if afar they took their point of sight, 85
And distant things, as intimately deep
As if they touched them. Let us strive for this.
I do distrust the poet who discerns
No character or glory in his times,
And trundles back his soul five hundred years, 90
Past moat and drawbridge, into a castle-court,
Oh not to sing of lizards or of toads
Alive i' the ditch there, – 'twere excusable;
But of some black chief, half knight, half sheep-lifter,
Some beauteous dame, half chattel and half queen, 95
As dead as must be, for the greater part,
The poems made on their chivalric bones;
And that's no wonder: death inherits death.
Nay, if there's room for poets in the world
A little overgrown, (I think there is), 100
Their sole work is to represent the age,
Their age, not Charlemagne's,⋄ – this live, throbbing age,
That brawls, cheats, maddens, calculates, aspires,
And spends more passion, more heroic heat,

Betwixt the mirrors of its drawing-rooms,   105
Than Roland with his knights, at Roncesvalles.°
To flinch from modern varnish, coat or flounce,
Cry out for togas and the picturesque
Is fatal, – foolish too. King Arthur's self
Was commonplace to Lady Guenever;   110
And Camelot to minstrels seemed as flat,
As Regent Street to poets.

Flush or Faunus (1850)

Elizabeth Barrett Browning was devoted to her cocker spaniel, Flush, even paying ransom money for him when he was kidnapped by dog-snatchers in London. He went with the Brownings to Italy, where he died of old age.

Virginia Woolf's short novel, *Flush* (1933), ends with this poem. The novel is Flush's life story. In telling it, Woolf also tells the romantic story of the Brownings' courtship, marriage and life in Italy.

✦ *Activities*

1 Make a spider chart which shows the range of subject matter and styles in this selection of Elizabeth Barrett Browning's poems: politics; poetry; love; sonnets; blank verse …

2 Whatever her subject matter, Elizabeth Barrett Browning's poems are full of strong feelings. Choose a subject about which you feel strongly, personally or politically, and write the opening lines (if you decide to write in verse), or paragraph (if you decide to write prose).

    a Compare your methods of expressing your feelings with hers.

    b Redraft your piece in the style of one of Elizabeth Barrett Browning's poems.

Flush or Faunus

You see this dog. It was but yesterday
I mused forgetful of his presence here
Till thought on thought drew downward tear on tear:
When from the pillow, where wet-cheeked I lay,
A head as hairy as Faunus,◇ thrust its way   5
Right sudden against my face, – two golden clear
Large eyes astonished mine, – a drooping ear
Did flap me on either cheek, to dry the spray!
I started first, as some Arcadian,◇
Amazed by goatly God in twilight grove: 10
But as my bearded vision closelier ran
My tears off, I knew Flush, and rose above
Surprise and sadness; thanking the true PAN,◇
Who, by low creatures, leads to heights of love.

Robert Browning (1812–1889)

Browning wrote one of the best descriptions of his own poetry in the final poem of his collection *Men and Women*. The poem is called 'One word more', and is addressed to Elizabeth Barrett Browning; in it he says:

> Love, you saw me gather men and women,
> Live or dead or fashioned by my fancy,
> Enter each and all, and use their service,
> Speak from every mouth, – the speech a poem.

Browning's speciality is the dramatic monologue – a poem which reveals the character, personality and situation of the speaker through what that person says and the way they say it.

Porphyria's Lover (1836)
My Last Duchess (1842)
The Laboratory (1845)

In these poems, Browning has invented three sinister characters, in three different settings. 'Porphyria's Lover' is not specific about the period when it is set, but the sub-title, Ferrara, for 'My Last Duchess', suggests sixteenth-century Italy and the 'Ancien régime', for 'The Laboratory', suggests a corrupt royal court in the eighteenth century.

✦ *Activity*
The poems contain all the clues you need to work out:
- who is speaking
- what sort of a person each speaker is
- what the situation is.

a In each poem a crime has been (or in the case of 'The Laboratory' is about to be) committed. Half the class should represent the detective on the case, and the other half the lawyer for the defence. In pairs, collect:
  • the evidence for the prosecution
  • the evidence and arguments which you will use to save your client from the death penalty.

b Role play the trial. Prosecution and defence can have two or three supporting detectives and lawyers to assist. You will also need judge and jury, and a small group to check that any evidence is soundly based in the poem.

Porphyria's Lover

The rain set early in tonight, *a*
  The sullen wind was soon awake, *b*
It tore the elm-tops down for spite, *a*
  And did its worst to vex the lake: *b*
  I listened with heart fit to break. *b*   5
When glided in Porphyria; straight *b*
  She shut the cold out and the storm, *c*
And kneeled and made the cheerless grate *d*
  Blaze up, and all the cottage warm; *c*
  Which done, she rose, and from her form *c*   10
Withdrew the dripping cloak and shawl, *e*
  And laid her soiled gloves by, untied *f*
Her hat and let the damp hair fall, *e*
  And, last, she sat down by my side *f*
  And called me. When no voice replied, *f*   15
She put my arm about her waist,
  And made her smooth white shoulder bare,
And all her yellow hair displaced,
  And, stooping, made my cheek lie there,
  And spread, o'er all, her yellow hair,   20
Murmuring how she loved me – she
  Too weak, for all her heart's endeavour,
To set its struggling passion free
  From pride, and vainer ties dissever, *
  And give herself to me for ever.   25
But passion sometimes would prevail,
  Nor could tonight's gay feast restrain
A sudden thought of one so pale
  For love of her, and all in vain:
  So, she was come through wind and rain.   30
Be sure I looked up at her eyes
  Happy and proud; at last I knew
Porphyria worshipped me; surprise
  Made my heart swell, and still it grew

While I debated what to do.   35
That moment she was mine, mine, fair,
   Perfectly pure and good: I found
A thing to do, and all her hair
   In one long yellow string I wound
   Three times her little throat around,   40
And strangled her. No pain felt she;
     I am quite sure she felt no pain.
As a shut bud that holds a bee,
   I warily oped her lids: again
   Laughed the blue eyes without a stain.   45
And I untightened next the tress
   About her neck; her cheek once more
Blushed bright beneath my burning kiss:
   I propped her head up as before,
   Only, this time my shoulder bore   50
Her head, which droops upon it still:
   The smiling rosy little head,
So glad it has its utmost will,
   That all it scorned at once is fled,
   And I, its love, am gained instead!   55
Porphyria's love: she guessed not how
   Her darling one wish would be heard.
And thus we sit together now,
   And all night long we have not stirred,
   And yet God has not said a word!   60

My Last Duchess
Ferrara

That's my last Duchess painted on the wall,
Looking as if she were alive. I call
That piece a wonder, now: Fra◇ Pandolf's hands
Worked busily a day, and there she stands.
Will't please you sit and look at her? I said   5
'Fra Pandolf' by design, for never read
Strangers like you that pictured countenance,
The depth and passion of its earnest glance,
But to myself they turned (since none puts by
The curtain I have drawn for you, but I)   10
And seemed as they would ask me, if they durst,
How such a glance came there; so, not the first
Are you to turn and ask thus. Sir, 'twas not
Her husband's presence only, called that spot
Of joy into the Duchess' cheek: perhaps   15
Fra Pandolf chanced to say 'Her mantle laps
Over my lady's wrist too much,' or 'Paint
Must never hope to reproduce the faint
Half-flush that dies along her throat': such stuff
Was courtesy, she thought, and cause enough   20
For calling up that spot of joy. She had
A heart – how shall I say? – too soon made glad,
Too easily impressed; she liked whate'er
She looked on, and her looks went everywhere.
Sir, 'twas all one! My favour◇ at her breast,   25
The dropping of the daylight in the West,
The bough of cherries some officious fool
Broke in the orchard for her, the white mule
She rode with round the terrace – all and each
Would draw from her alike the approving speech,   30
Or blush, at least. She thanked men, – good! but thanked
Somehow – I know not how – as if she ranked
My gift of a nine-hundred-years-old name

With anybody's gift. Who'd stoop to blame
This sort of trifling? Even had you skill   35
In speech – (which I have not) – to make your will
Quite clear to such an one, and say, 'Just this
Or that in you disgusts me; here you miss,
Or there exceed the mark' – and if she let
Herself be lessoned so, nor plainly set   40
Her wits to yours, forsooth, and made excuse,
– E'en then would be some stooping; and I choose
Never to stoop. Oh sir, she smiled, no doubt,
Whene'er I passed her; but who passed without
Much the same smile? This grew; I gave commands;   45
Then all smiles stopped together. There she stands
As if alive. Will't please you rise? We'll meet
The company below, then. I repeat,
The Count your master's known munificence
Is ample warrant that no just pretence   50
Of mine for dowry will be disallowed;
Though his fair daughter's self, as I avowed
At starting, is my object. Nay, we'll go
Together down, sir. Notice Neptune, though,
Taming a sea-horse, thought a rarity,   55
Which Claus of Innsbruck cast in bronze for me!

The Laboratory
Ancien Régime

I

Now that I, tying thy glass mask tightly,
May gaze thro' these faint smokes curling whitely,
As thou pliest thy trade in this devil's-smithy –
Which is the poison to poison her, prithee?

II

He is with her, and they know that I know   5
Where they are, what they do: they believe my tears flow
While they laugh, laugh at me, at me fled to the drear
Empty church, to pray God in, for them! – I am here.

III

Grind away, moisten and mash up thy paste,
Pound at thy powder – I am not in haste!   10
Better sit thus, and observe thy strange things,
Than go where men wait me and dance at the King's.

IV

That in the mortar – you call it a gum?
Ah, the brave tree whence such gold oozings come!
And yonder soft phial, the exquisite blue,   15
Sure to taste sweetly, – is that poison too?

V

Had I but all of them, thee and thy treasures,
What a wild crowd of invisible pleasures!
To carry pure death in an earring, a casket,
A signet, a fan-mount, a filigree basket!   20

VI

Soon, at the King's, a mere lozenge to give,
And Pauline should have just thirty minutes to live!
But to light a pastile, and Elise, with her head
And her breast and her arms and her hands, should drop dead!

VII

Quick – is it finished? The colour's too grim!   25
Why not soft like the phial's, enticing and dim?
Let it brighten her drink, let her turn it and stir,
And try it and taste, ere she fix and prefer!

VIII

What a drop! She's not little, no minion like me!
That's why she ensnared him: this never will free   30
The soul from those masculine eyes, – say, 'no!'
To that pulse's magnificent come-and-go.

IX

For only last night, as they whispered, I brought
My own eyes to bear on her so, that I thought
Could I keep them one half minute fixed, she would fall   35
Shrivelled; she fell not; yet this does it all!

X

Not that I bid you spare her the pain;
Let death be felt and the proof remain:
Brand, burn up, bite into its grace –
He is sure to remember her dying face!   40

XI

Is it done? Take my mask off! Nay, be not morose;
It kills her, and this prevents seeing it close:
The delicate droplet, my whole fortune's fee!
If it hurts her, beside, can it ever hurt me?

XII

Now, take all my jewels, gorge gold to your fill,   45
You may kiss me, old man, on my mouth if you will!
But brush this dust off me, lest horror it brings
Ere I know it – next moment I dance at the King's!

from The Bishop Orders his Tomb at Saint Praxed's Church (1845)

Most of Browning's later dramatic monologues are the length readers today expect of a short story, rather than a poem. This extract gives you the first half of the whole poem. Saint Praxed's Church does not exist; Browning has invented it and the Bishop. John Ruskin (1819–1900), a contemporary art historian and critic who did not always find Browning's poems easy to understand, praised this one, saying:

> I know of no other piece of modern English, prose
> or poetry, in which there is so much told ... of the
> Renaissance spirit – its worldliness, inconsistency,
> pride, hypocrisy, ignorance of itself, love of art, of
> luxury ...
>
> (*Modern Painters* Vol IV, 1856)

✦ *Activities*

1 The Seven Deadly Sins are: Pride, Wrath, Envy, Lust, Gluttony, Avarice, Sloth. How many of these do you think the Bishop has committed?

2 Write an obituary for the Bishop either by one of his fellow bishops, or by a disapproving member of his congregation.

The Bishop Orders his Tomb at Saint Praxed's Church

Rome, 15—

Vanity,◇ saith the preacher, vanity!
Draw round my bed: is Anselm keeping back?
Nephews – sons mine … ah God, I know not! Well –
She, men would have to be your mother once,
Old Gandolf envied me, so fair she was!   5
What's done is done, and she is dead beside,
Dead long ago, and I am Bishop since,
And as she died so must we die ourselves,
And thence ye may perceive the world's a dream.
Life, how and what is it? As here I lie   10
In this state-chamber, dying by degrees,
Hours and long hours in the dead night, I ask
'Do I live, am I dead?' Peace, peace seems all.
Saint Praxed's ever was the church for peace;
And so, about this tomb of mine. I fought   15
With tooth and nail to save my niche, ye know:
– Old Gandolf cozened◇ me, despite my care;
Shrewd was that snatch from out the corner South
He graced his carrion with, God curse the same!
Yet still my niche is not so cramped but thence   20
One sees the pulpit o' the epistle-side,
And somewhat of the choir, those silent seats,
And up into the airy dome where live
The angels, and a sunbeam's sure to lurk:
And I shall fill my slab of basalt◇ there,   25
And 'neath my tabernacle take my rest,
With those nine columns round me, two and two,
The odd one at my feet where Anselm stands:
Peach-blossom marble all, the rare, the ripe
As fresh-poured red wine of a mighty pulse.   30
– Old Gandolf with his paltry onion-stone,◇
Put me where I may look at him! True peach,

Rosy and flawless: how I earned the prize!
Draw close: that conflagration of my church
– What then? So much was saved if aught were missed! 35
My sons, ye would not be my death? Go dig
The white-grape vineyard where the oil-press stood,
Drop water gently till the surface sink,
And if ye find ... Ah God, I know not, I! ...
Bedded in store of rotten fig-leaves soft, 40
And corded up in a tight olive-frail,◇
Some lump, ah God, of *lapis lazuli*,◇
Big as a Jew's head cut off at the nape,
Blue as a vein o'er the Madonna's breast ...
Sons, all have I bequeathed you, villas, all, 45
That brave Frascati villa with its bath,
So, let the blue lump poise between my knees,
Like God the Father's globe on both his hands
Ye worship in the Jesu Church so gay,
For Gandolf shall not choose but see and burst! 50
Swift as a weaver's shuttle fleet our years:
Man goeth to the grave, and where is he?
Did I say basalt for my slab, sons? Black –
'Twas ever antique-black I meant! How else
Shall ye contrast my frieze to come beneath? 55
The bas-relief◇ in bronze ye promised me,
Those Pans and Nymphs ye wot of, and perchance
Some tripod, thyrsus,◇ with a vase or so,
The Saviour at his sermon on the mount,
Saint Praxed in a glory, and one Pan 60
Ready to twitch the Nymph's last garment off,
And Moses with the tables◇ ... but I know
Ye mark me not! What do they whisper thee,
Child of my bowels, Anselm? Ah, ye hope
To revel down my villas while I gasp 65
Bricked o'er with beggar's mouldy travertine◇
Which Gandolf from his tomb-top chuckles at!

Fra Lippo Lippi *and* Andrea del Sarto

Browning was interested in Italian art and artists; he drew himself and made art the subject of several of his poems. Fra Lippo Lippi (1406–1469) and Andrea del Sarto (1486–1530) were real people, who lived and worked in Florence. These descriptions of them are from Giorgio Vasari's *Lives of the Artists*, first published in the 1550s.

FRA FILIPPO DI TOMMASO LIPPI, a Carmelite, was born in Florence, in a street called Ardiglione, below the Canto alla Cucilia and behind the Carmelite Convent. The death of his father left him, at the age of two, a sad and solitary orphan, since his mother had died not long after he was born. He was put under the care of his aunt, Mona Lapaccia, Tommaso's sister, but she found it a struggle to bring him up and, when she could no longer manage, sent him, at the age of eight, to be a friar in the Carmelite Convent. At the convent he showed himself dexterous and ingenious in any work he had to do with his hands, but equally dull and incapable of learning when it came to his books; so he never spent any time studying his letters, which he regarded with great distaste. The boy (who was called by his secular name, Filippo) was placed with the other novices in the charge of the master teaching grammar to see what he could learn; but instead of studying he spent all his time scrawling pictures on his own books and those of others, and so eventually the prior decided to give him every chance and opportunity of learning to paint.

It is said that Fra Filippo was so lustful that he would give anything to enjoy a woman he wanted if he thought he could have his way; and if he couldn't buy what he wanted, then he would cool his passion by painting her portrait and reasoning with himself. His lust was so violent that when it took hold of him he could never concentrate on his work. And because of this, one time or other when he was doing something for Cosimo de' Medici in Cosimo's house, Cosimo had him locked in so that he wouldn't wander away and waste time. After he had been confined for a few days, Fra Filippo's amorous or rather his animal desires drove him one night to seize a pair of scissors, make a rope from his bed-sheets and escape through a window to pursue his own pleasures for days on end. When Cosimo discovered that he was gone, he searched for him and eventually got him back to work. And after that he always allowed him to come and go as he liked, having regretted the way he had shut him up before and realizing how dangerous it was for such a madman to be confined. Cosimo determined for the future to keep a hold on him by affection and kindness and, being served all the more readily, he used to say that artists of genius were to be treated with respect, not used as hacks.

ANDREA DEL SARTO, most excellent Florentine painter, 1486–1530. We have now come, after the lives of so many craftsmen who have been outstanding, some for colouring, some for drawing, and others for invention, to the most excellent Andrea del Sarto, in whose single person Nature and art showed all that painting can achieve by means of drawing, colouring and invention: and indeed if Andrea had possessed a little more boldness and daring of spirit, to match his very profound judgement and talent as a painter, he would, there is no doubt at all, have been without equal. But a certain timidity of spirit, along with a sort of abjectness and simplicity of character, never let there be seen in him the kind of lively ardour or the boldness which, added to his other attributes, would have made him truly inspired in his work; and so for this reason he lacked those adornments, that grandeur and copiousness of styles, which are seen in many other painters. None the less his figures, despite their simplicity and purity, were well conceived, without errors, and in all respects utterly perfect. The expressions of the faces he painted, whether boys or women, are natural and graceful, and those of his men, both young and old, are done with vivacity and splendid animation while his draperies are a beauty to behold, and his nudes are very well conceived. And although he drew with simplicity, his colours are none the less rare and truly inspired.

Fra Lippo Lippi

This extract is the first half of the whole poem. Fra Lippo Lippi tells you how he became a monk; he also tells you what sort of a painter he is, and what he is trying to achieve as an artist.

✦ *Activity*

One reason why Browning's long poems are hard to read is their unbroken appearance on the page. If this poem was divided into paragraphs, like a story in prose, it would be much easier to deal with. Another reason why Browning's poetry is often hard to read is that he writes extremely long sentences.

a Work through the first fifty lines with a partner, and decide where you would start new paragraphs. Give each of your paragraphs a headline, for example:

- lines 1–6: Monk caught by nightwatch!
- lines 7–11: He tells them how to do their job!

b On a copy of lines 58–135, highlight the events Fra Lippo Lippi describes there which match with details in the extract from Vasari's *Lives*.

c In a group of five or six, read lines 143–162 together round the group, with each person reading just to the next punctuation mark. (This will mean that someone may get a single word, someone else may get several lines.) You will find this is a useful technique to use when reading all sorts of poetry, because it will help you to pay more attention to the ways in which poets use punctuation, and see the difference between reading line by line, and reading the bigger units of meaning which make up the poem. Before you start you could work out which bit you will be saying, so that you can concentrate more on how Browning is putting the sentence together and what he is describing.

d Look at lines 163–201. With a partner, work out where in the poem Fra Lippo Lippi is speaking, and where he is repeating what other people say. Join with one or two other pairs; in the larger group discuss:

- what the monks admire about his painting
- what the Prior and the learned people think about his painting
- what Fra Lippo Lippi thinks of their opinions
- what you think he wants to achieve, as an artist.

from *Fra Lippo Lippi*

I am poor brother Lippo, by your leave!
You need not clap your torches to my face.
Zooks, what's to blame? you think you see a monk!
What, 'tis past midnight, and you go the rounds,
And here you catch me at an alley's end   5
Where sportive ladies leave their doors ajar?
The Carmine's⬦ my cloister: hunt it up,
Do, – harry out, if you must show your zeal,
Whatever rat, there, haps on his wrong hole,
And nip each softling of a wee white mouse,   10
Weke, weke, that's crept to keep him company!
Aha, you know your betters! Then, you'll take
Your hand away that's fiddling on my throat,
And please to know me likewise. Who am I?
Why, one, sir, who is lodging with a friend   15
Three streets off – he's a certain ... how d'ye call?
Master – a ... Cosimo of the Medici,⬦
I' the house that caps the corner. Boh! you were best!
Remember and tell me, the day you're hanged,
How you affected such a gullet's-gripe!   20
But you, sir, it concerns you that your knaves
Pick up a manner nor discredit you:
Zooks, are we pilchards, that they sweep the streets
And count fair prize what comes into their net?
He's Judas to a tittle,⬦ that man is!   25
Just such a face! Why, sir, you make amends.
Lord, I'm not angry! Bid your hangdogs go
Drink out this quarter-florin to the health
Of the munificent House that harbours me
(And many more beside, lads! more beside!)   30
And all's come square again. I'd like his face –
His, elbowing on his comrade in the door
With the pike and lantern, – for the slave that holds
John Baptist's head a-dangle by the hair

With one hand ('Look you, now,' as who should say)   35
And his weapon in the other, yet unwiped!
It's not your chance to have a bit of chalk,
A wood-coal or the like? or you should see!
Yes, I'm the painter, since you style me so.
What, brother Lippo's doings, up and down,   40
You know them and they take you? like enough!
I saw the proper twinkle in your eye –
'Tell you, I liked your looks at very first.
Let's sit and set things straight now, hip to haunch.
Here's spring come, and the nights one makes up bands   45
To roam the town and sing out carnival,
And I've been three weeks shut within my mew,°
A-painting for the great man, saints and saints
And saints again. I could not paint all night –
Ouf! I leaned out of window for fresh air.   50
There came a hurry of feet and little feet,
A sweep of lute-strings, laughs, and whifts of song, –
Flower o' the broom,
Take away love, and our earth is a tomb!
Flower o' the quince,   55
I let Lisa go, and what good in life since?
Flower o' the thyme – and so on. Round they went.
Scarce had they turned the corner when a titter
Like the skipping of rabbits by moonlight, – three slim shapes,
And a face that looked up … zooks, sir, flesh and blood,   60
That's all I'm made of! Into shreds it went,
Curtain and counterpane and coverlet,
All the bed-furniture – a dozen knots,
There was a ladder! Down I let myself,
Hands and feet, scrambling somehow, and so dropped,   65
And after them. I came up with the fun
Hard by Saint Laurence, hail fellow, well met, –
Flower o' the rose,
If I've been merry, what matter who knows?
And so as I was stealing back again   70
To get to bed and have a bit of sleep
Ere I rise up tomorrow and go work

On Jerome knocking at his poor old breast
With his great round stone to subdue the flesh,
You snap me of the sudden. Ah, I see!   75
Though your eye twinkles still, you shake your head –
Mine's shaved – a monk, you say – the sting's in that!
If Master Cosimo announced himself,
Mum's the word naturally; but a monk!
Come, what am I a beast for? tell us, now!   80
I was a baby when my mother died
And father died and left me in the street.
I starved there, God knows how, a year or two
On fig-skins, melon-parings, rinds and shucks,[◇]
Refuse and rubbish. One fine frosty day,   85
My stomach being empty as your hat,
The wind doubled me up and down I went.
Old Aunt Lapaccia trussed me with one hand,
(Its fellow was a stinger as I knew)
And so along the wall, over the bridge,   90
By the straight cut to the convent. Six words there,
While I stood munching my first bread that month:
'So, boy, you're minded,' quoth the good fat father
Wiping his own mouth, 'twas refection-time, –
'To quit this very miserable world?   95
Will you renounce' … 'the mouthful of bread?' thought I;
By no means! Brief, they made a monk of me;
I did renounce the world, its pride and greed,
Palace, farm, villa, shop and banking-house,
Trash, such as these poor devils of Medici   100
Have given their hearts to – all at eight years old.
Well, sir, I found in time, you may be sure,
'Twas not for nothing – the good bellyful,
The warm serge and the rope that goes all round,
And day-long blessed idleness beside!   105
'Let's see what the urchin's fit for' – that came next.
Not overmuch their way, I must confess.
Such a to-do! They tried me with their books:
Lord, they'd have taught me Latin in pure waste!
Flower o' the clove,   110

All the Latin I construe is, 'amo' I love!
But, mind you, when a boy starves in the streets
Eight years together, as my fortune was,
Watching folk's faces to know who will fling
The bit of half-stripped grape-bunch he desires,   115
And who will curse or kick him for his pains, –
Which gentleman processional and fine,
Holding a candle to the Sacrament,
Will wink and let him lift a plate and catch
The droppings of the wax to sell again,   120
Or holla for the Eight° and have him whipped, –
How say I? – nay, which dog bites, which lets drop
His bone from the heap of offal in the street, –
Why, soul and sense of him grow sharp alike,
He learns the look of things, and none the less   125
For admonition from the hunger-pinch.
I had a store of such remarks, be sure,
Which, after I found leisure, turned to use.
I drew men's faces on my copy-books,
Scrawled them within the antiphonary's° marge,   130
Joined legs and arms to the long music-notes,
Found eyes and nose and chin for A's and B's,
And made a string of pictures of the world
Betwixt the ins and outs of verb and noun,
On the wall, the bench, the door. The monks looked black.   135
'Nay,' quoth the Prior, 'turn him out, d'ye say?
In no wise. Lose a crow and catch a lark.
What if at last we get our man of parts,
We Carmelites, like those Camaldolese
And Preaching Friars, to do our church up fine   140
And put the front on it that ought to be!'
And hereupon he bade me daub away.
Thank you! my head being crammed, the walls a blank,
Never was such prompt disemburdening.
First, every sort of monk, the black and white,   145
I drew them, fat and lean: then, folk at church,
From good old gossips waiting to confess
Their cribs of barrel-droppings, candle-ends, –

To the breathless fellow at the altar-foot,
Fresh from his murder, safe and sitting there   150
With the little children round him in a row
Of admiration, half for his beard and half
For that white anger of his victim's son
Shaking a fist at him with one fierce arm,
Signing himself with the other because of Christ   155
(Whose sad face on the cross sees only this
After the passion of a thousand years)
Till some poor girl, her apron o'er her head,
(Which the intense eyes looked through) came at eve
On tiptoe, said a word, dropped in a loaf,   160
Her pair of earrings and a bunch of flowers
(The brute took growling), prayed, and so was gone.
I painted all, then cried ''Tis ask and have;
Choose, for more's ready!' – laid the ladder flat,
And showed my covered bit of cloister-wall.   165
The monks closed in a circle and praised loud
Till checked, taught what to see and not to see,
Being simple bodies, – 'That's the very man!
Look at the boy who stoops to pat the dog!
That woman's like the Prior's niece who comes   170
To care about his asthma: it's the life!'
But there my triumph's straw-fire flared and funked;
Their betters took their turn to see and say:
The Prior and the learned pulled a face
And stopped all that in no time. 'How? what's here?   175
Quite from the mark of painting, bless us all!
Faces, arms, legs and bodies like the true
As much as pea and pea! it's devil's-game!
Your business is not to catch men with show,
With homage to the perishable clay,   180
But lift them over it, ignore it all,
Make them forget there's such a thing as flesh.
Your business is to paint the souls of men –
Man's soul, and it's a fire, smoke ... no, it's not ...
It's vapour done up like a new-born babe –   185
(In that shape when you die it leaves your mouth)

It's … well, what matters talking, it's the soul!
Give us no more of body than shows soul!
Here's Giotto, with his Saint a-praising God,
That sets us praising, – why not stop with him?   190
Why put all thoughts of praise out of our head
With wonder at lines, colours, and what not?
Paint the soul, never mind the legs and arms!
Rub all out, try at it a second time.
Oh, that white smallish female with the breasts,   195
She's just my niece … Herodias, I would say, –
Who went and danced and got men's heads cut off!
Have it all out!' Now, is this sense, I ask?
A fine way to paint soul, by painting body
So ill, the eye can't stop there, must go further   200
And can't fare worse!

Andrea del Sarto

These extracts are the beginning and the end of the poem. In it Andrea del Sarto is speaking to his wife, Lucrezia; he talks about his painting, compares himself unfavourably to the other great artists working in Florence – Raphael, Michelangelo and Leonardo da Vinci – and reminisces about the time he spent as a successful painter at the French court, before Lucrezia made him return to Italy.

Browning's skill as a writer of dramatic monologues lies in the way in which he gradually reveals a character and a situation as the poem develops. From Vasari, you can learn that Andrea del Sarto was an excellent painter, extremely skilful in drawing and in the use of colour. From Browning's poem you can also deduce his relationship with his wife and the reasons for it, his state of mind, and how he feels about himself as an artist.

✦ *Activity*

Remember that Vasari would have spent a lot of time with Andrea del Sarto. Use the information you gain from reading these selected parts of the poem to write a continuation of the extract from Vasari's *Lives* (p. 119), in which you describe del Sarto's marriage, and his feelings about himself and his art. As you can see from the life of Fra Lippo Lippi (pp. 117–118), Vasari writes in a very informal way, and is not afraid of making personal remarks about his subjects and their behaviour. Use the extracts as a model for your piece of writing.

from *Andrea del Sarto*
(Called 'The Faultless Painter')

But do not let us quarrel any more,
No, my Lucrezia; bear with me for once:
Sit down and all shall happen as you wish.
You turn your face, but does it bring your heart?
I'll work then for your friend's friend, never fear,   5
Treat his own subject after his own way,
Fix his own time, accept too his own price,
And shut the money into this small hand
When next it takes mine. Will it? tenderly?
Oh, I'll content him, – but tomorrow, Love!   10
I often am much wearier than you think,
This evening more than usual, and it seems
As if – forgive now – should you let me sit
Here by the window with your hand in mine
And look a half-hour forth on Fiesole,$^{\diamond}$ 15
Both of one mind, as married people use,
Quietly, quietly the evening through,
I might get up tomorrow to my work
Cheerful and fresh as ever. Let us try.
Tomorrow, how you shall be glad for this!   20
Your soft hand is a woman of itself,
And mine the man's bared breast she curls inside.
Don't count the time lost, neither; you must serve
For each of the five pictures we require:
It saves a model. So! keep looking so –   25
My serpentining beauty, rounds on rounds!
– How could you ever prick those perfect ears,
Even to put the pearl there! oh, so sweet –
My face, my moon, my everybody's moon,
Which everybody looks on and calls his,   30
And, I suppose, is looked on by in turn,
While she looks – no one's: very dear, no less.
You smile? why, there's my picture ready made,

There's what we painters call our harmony!
A common greyness silvers everything, –   35
All in a twilight, you and I alike
– You, at the point of your first pride in me
(That's gone you know), – but I, at every point;
My youth, my hope, my art, being all toned down
To yonder sober pleasant Fiesole.   40
There's the bell clinking from the chapel-top;
That length of convent-wall across the way
Holds the trees safer, huddled more inside;
The last monk leaves the garden; days decrease,
And autumn grows, autumn in everything.   45
Eh? the whole seems to fall into a shape
As if I saw alike my work and self
And all that I was born to be and do,
A twilight-piece.

                        *   *   *   *   *   *

This hour has been an hour! Another smile?   50
If you would sit thus by me every night
I should work better, do you comprehend?
I mean that I should earn more, give you more.
See, it is settled dusk now; there's a star;
Morello's◊ gone, the watch-lights show the wall,   55
The cue-owls speak the name we call them by.
Come from the window, love, – come in, at last,
Inside the melancholy little house
We built to be so gay with. God is just.
King Francis may forgive me: oft at nights   60
When I look up from painting, eyes tired out,
The walls become illumined, brick from brick
Distinct, instead of mortar, fierce bright gold,
That gold of his I did cement them with!
Let us but love each other. Must you go?   65
That Cousin here again? he waits outside?
Must see you – you, and not with me? Those loans?
More gaming debts to pay? you smiled for that?

Well, let smiles buy me! have you more to spend?
While hand and eye and something of a heart   70
Are left me, work's my ware, and what's it worth?
I'll pay my fancy. Only let me sit
The grey remainder of the evening out,
Idle, you call it, and muse perfectly
How I could paint, were I but back in France,   75
One picture, just one more – the Virgin's face,
Not yours this time! I want you at my side
To hear them – that is, Michel Agnolo◇ –
Judge all I do and tell you of its worth.
Will you? Tomorrow, satisfy your friend.   80
I take the subjects for his corridor,
Finish the portrait out of hand – there, there,
And throw him in another thing or two
If he demurs; the whole should prove enough
To pay for this same Cousin's freak. Beside,   85
What's better and what's all I care about,
Get you the thirteen scudi for the ruff!
Love, does that please you? Ah, but what does he,
The Cousin! what does he to please you more?   90

    I am grown peaceful as old age tonight.
I regret little, I would change still less.
Since there my past life lies, why alter it?
The very wrong to Francis! – it is true
I took his coin, was tempted and complied,   95
And built this house and sinned, and all is said.
My father and my mother died of want.
Well, had I riches of my own? you see
How one gets rich! Let each one bear his lot.
They were born poor, lived poor, and poor they died: 100
And I have laboured somewhat in my time
And not been paid profusely. Some good son
Paint my two hundred pictures – let him try!

No doubt, there's something strikes a balance. Yes,
You loved me quite enough, it seems tonight.   105
This must suffice me here. What would one have?
In heaven, perhaps, new chances, one more chance –
Four great walls in the New Jerusalem,
Meted on each side by the angel's reed,
For Leonard,◇ Rafael,◇ Agnolo and me   110
To cover – the three first without a wife,
While I have mine! So – still they overcome
Because there's still Lucrezia, – as I choose.

Again the Cousin's whistle! Go, my Love.

'Childe Roland to the Dark Tower Came' (1855)

You will find Edgar's song at the end of Act III scene 4 of Shakespeare's *King Lear*.

> Childe Rowland to the dark tower came,
> His word was still – Fie, foh and fum
>   I smell the blood of a British man.

Edgar is pretending to be a mad beggar, and the scene takes place on a deserted heath in a storm. Apart from aspects of their settings, and the first line of the 'song', there are no other obvious connections between Browning's poem and Shakespeare's play.

Because people often found Browning's poems difficult to understand they frequently asked him what he had meant when he wrote them, but he didn't usually give very straightforward answers. Asked about this poem in 1887, thirty years after it was written, he said:

> I was conscious of no allegorical intention in writing it … Childe Roland came upon me as a kind of dream. I had to write it then and there, and I finished it the same day, I believe. But it was simply that I had to do it. I did not know then what I meant beyond that, and I'm sure I don't know now. But I am very fond of it.

✦ *Activities*

1 Before you begin to read the poem, brainstorm your associations with the following:
   - King Arthur and his knights
   - the sort of countryside or landscape you might see in a nightmare or a horror film
   - the sort of people or creatures you might meet in this landscape
   - the colours, sounds and sights you associate with nightmare and horror.

2 Using collage or drawings, make a visual version of 'Childe Roland'. You will need to create story boards in small groups, working out how many separate illustrations you will need to tell the 'story', and what details you think must be included. When you have agreed the final number and sequence of images as a class, divide into small groups or pairs to produce one or two images as part of the whole class version. (Alternatively, make different possible versions and compare them.)

3 When the visual versions are complete, re-read the poem aloud. Discuss what, if anything, you think is missing from your versions of Browning's poem, or what you might have added to them. Do you think you have succeeded in conveying the atmosphere and the state of mind of the speaker? Now speculate about why you think Browning was 'very fond' of this poem.

'Childe◇ Roland to the Dark Tower Came'
(See Edgar's song in Lear)

I

My first thought was, he lied in every word,
   That hoary cripple, with malicious eye
   Askance to watch the working of his lie
On mine, and mouth scarce able to afford
Suppression of the glee, that pursed and scored   5
   Its edge, at one more victim gained thereby.

II

What else should he be set for, with his staff?
   What, save to waylay with his lies, ensnare
   All travellers who might find him posted there,
And ask the road? I guessed what skull-like laugh   10
Would break, what crutch 'gin write my epitaph
   For pastime in the dusty thoroughfare,

III

If at his counsel I should turn aside
   Into that ominous tract which, all agree,
   Hides the Dark Tower. Yet acquiescingly   15
I did turn as he pointed: neither pride
Nor hope rekindling at the end descried,
   So much as gladness that some end might be.

IV–VI

He broods on feelings of failure and depression.

VII

Thus, I had so long suffered in this quest,
   Heard failure prophesied so oft, been writ   20
   So many times among 'The Band' – to wit,

The knights who to the Dark Tower's search addressed
Their steps – that just to fail as they, seemed best,
   And all the doubt was now – should I be fit?

VIII–IX

The sun is setting as he starts his journey. Turning round, he
finds the cripple has vanished. He is completely alone.

X

So on I went. I think I never saw   25
   Such starved ignoble nature; nothing throve:
   For flowers – as well expect a cedar grove!
But cockle,⋄ spurge, according to their law
Might propagate their kind, with none to awe,
   You'd think; a burr had been a treasure-trove.   30

XI

No! Penury, inertness and grimace,
   In some strange sort were the land's portion. 'See
   Or shut your eyes,' said Nature peevishly,
'It nothing skills: I cannot help my case:
'Tis the Last Judgement's fire must cure this place,   35
   Calcine⋄ its clods and set my prisoners free.'

XII

If there pushed any ragged thistle-stalk
   Above its mates, the head was chopped; the bents⋄
   Were jealous else. What made those holes and rents
In the dock's harsh swarth leaves, bruised as to balk   40
All hope of greenness? 'tis a brute must walk
   Pashing their life out, with a brute's intents.

XIII

As for the grass, it grew as scant as hair
   In leprosy; thin dry blades pricked the mud
   Which underneath looked kneaded up with blood.   45

One stiff blind horse, his every bone a-stare,
Stood stupefied, however he came there:
    Thrust out past service from the devil's stud!

XIV

Alive? He might be dead for aught I know,
    With that read gaunt and collapsed neck a-strain,   50
    And shut eyes underneath the rusty mane;
Seldom went such grotesqueness with such woe;
I never saw a brute I hated so;
    He must be wicked to deserve such pain.

XV

I shut my eyes and turned them on my heart.   55
    As a man calls for wine before he fights,
    I asked one draught of earlier, happier sights,
Ere fitly I could hope to play my part.
Think first, fight afterwards – the soldier's art:
    One taste of the old time sets all to rights.   60

XVI

Not it! I fancied Cuthbert's reddening face
    Beneath its garniture of curly gold,
    Dear fellow, till I almost felt him fold
An arm in mine to fix me to the place,
That way he used. Alas, one night's disgrace!   65
    Out went my heart's new fire and left it cold.

XVII

Giles then, the soul of honour – there he stands
    Frank as ten years ago when knighted first.
    What honest man should dare (he said) he durst.
Good – but the scene shifts – faugh! what hangman-hands   70
Pin to his breast a parchment? His own bands
    Read it. Poor traitor, spit upon and curst!

XVIII

Better this present than a past like that;
    Back therefore to my darkening path again!
    No sound, no sight as far as eye could strain.   75
Will the night send a howlet°or a bat?
I asked: when something on the dismal flat
    Came to arrest my thoughts and change their train.

XIX

A sudden little river crossed my path
    As unexpected as a serpent comes.   80
    No sluggish tide congenial to the glooms;
This, as it frothed by, might have been a bath
For the fiend's glowing hoof – to see the wrath
    Of its black eddy bespate° with flakes and spumes.

XX

So petty yet so spiteful! All along,   85
    Low scrubby alders kneeled down over it;
    Drenched willows flung them headlong in a fit
Of mute despair, a suicidal throng:
The river which had done them all the wrong,
    Whate'er that was, rolled by, deterred no whit.   90

XXI

Which, while I forded, – good saints, how I feared
    To set my foot upon a dead man's cheek,
    Each step, or feel the spear I thrust to seek
For hollows, tangled in his hair or beard!
– It may have been a water-rat I speared,   95
    But, ugh! it sounded like a baby's shriek.

XXII–XXIV

Having crossed the river he finds himself in an even more frightful landscape.

XXV

Then came a bit of stubbed ground, once a wood,
　　Next a marsh, it would seem, and now mere earth
　　Desperate and done with; (so a fool finds mirth,
Makes a thing and then mars it, till his mood　　　　　　100
Changes and off he goes!) within a rood –
　　Bog, clay and rubble, sand and stark black dearth.

XXVI

Now blotches rankling, coloured gay and grim,
　　Now patches where some leanness of the soil's
　　Broke into moss or substances like boils;　　　　　　105
Then came some palsied oak, a cleft in him
Like a distorted mouth that splits its rim
　　Gaping at death, and dies while it recoils.

XXVII

And just as far as ever from the end!
　　Naught in the distance but the evening, naught　　　　110
　　To point my footstep further! At the thought,
A great black bird, Apollyon's◊ bosom-friend,
Sailed past, nor beat his wide wing dragon-penned
　　That brushed my cap – perchance the guide I sought.

XXVIII

For, looking up, aware I somehow grew,　　　　　　115
　　'Spite of the dusk, the plain had given place
　　All round to mountains – with such name to grace
Mere ugly heights and heaps now stolen in view.
How thus they had surprised me, – solve it, you!
　　How to get from them was no clearer case.　　　　　120

XXIX

Yet half I seemed to recognise some trick
　　Of mischief happened to me, God knows when –
　　In a bad dream perhaps. Here ended, then,
Progress this way. When, in the very nick
Of giving up, one time more, came a click　　　　　　125
　　As when a trap shuts – you're inside the den!

XXX

Burningly it came on me all at once,
    This was the place! those two hills on the right,
    Crouched like two bulls locked horn in horn in fight;
While to the left, a tall scalped mountain ... Dunce,   130
Dotard, a-dozing at the very nonce,[◇]
    After a life spent training for the sight!

XXXI

What in the midst lay but the Tower itself?
    The round squat turret, blind as the fool's heart,
    Built of brown stone, without a counterpart   135
In the whole world. The tempest's mocking elf
Points to the shipman thus the unseen shelf
    He strikes on, only when the timbers start.[◇]

XXXII

Not see? because of night perhaps? – why, day
    Came back again for that! before it left,   140
    The dying sunset kindled through a cleft:
The hills, like giants at a hunting, lay,
Chin upon hand, to see the game at bay, –
    'Now stab and end the creature – to the heft!'[◇]

XXXIII

Not hear? when noise was everywhere! it tolled   145
    Increasing like a bell. Names in my ears
    Of all the lost adventurers my peers, –
How such a one was strong, and such was bold,
And such was fortunate, yet each of old
    Lost, lost! one moment knelled the woe of years.   150

XXXIV

There they stood, ranged along the hill-sides, met
    To view the last of me, a living frame
    For one more picture! in a sheet of flame
I saw them and I knew them all. And yet
Dauntless the slug-horn[◇] to my lips I set,   155
    And blew. '*Childe Roland to the Dark Tower came.*'

Meeting at Night, Parting at Morning (1845)

Browning did not write many short poems, and did not often express personal feelings in his poetry, so these, although often found in anthologies, are not really typical of his work. However, you should still be able to recognise some characteristic features of Browning's poetry in the way they are written.

These poems were originally published as a single poem in two parts. Later Browning separated them and now you will often find 'Meeting at Night' on its own in anthologies.

✦ *Activity*

a Who do you think is the speaker in each of these poems?

b What do you think 'Parting at Morning' is about?

Your interpretation of 'Parting at Morning' is very likely to depend on that tiny word in line 3: 'him'. In 1889 Browning was asked whether the last line was 'an expression by her of her sense of loss of him, or the despairing cry of a ruined woman'. He answered:

> Neither: it is his confession of how fleeting is the belief [implied in 'Meeting at Night'] that such raptures are self-sufficient and enduring – as for the time they appear.

Although people still sometimes refer to ships or cars as 'she', this is a useful reminder that 'he' and 'him', 'she' and 'her' in Victorian poetry do not always refer to people. Here 'him' refers to the sun. (Who or what do you think 'she' refers to, in the penultimate line of 'De Gustibus'?)

Meeting at Night

The grey sea and the long black land;
And the yellow half-moon large and low;
And the startled little waves that leap
In fiery ringlets from their sleep,
As I gain the cove with pushing prow,   5
And quench its speed i' the slushy sand.

Then a mile of warm sea-scented beach;
Three fields to cross till a farm appears;
A tap at the pane, the quick sharp scratch
And blue spurt of a lighted match,   10
And a voice less loud, thro' its joys and fears,
Than the two hearts beating each to each!

Parting at Morning

Round the cape of a sudden came the sea,
And the sun looked over the mountain's rim;
And straight was a path of gold for him,
And the need of a world of men for me.

Home-Thoughts, from Abroad (1845)
De Gustibus – (1855)

'De gustibus non est disputandum' is a Latin saying which means 'There's no arguing about tastes'.

✦ *Activity*

Browning said about his poetry that his aim was to write:

> lyrics with more music and painting in them so as to
> get people to see and hear.

He did not mean 'music' and 'painting' to be taken literally when he said this, even though the characters in many of his poems are musicians and painters. He was referring to the importance for a reader of the sound of the poetry, and to the power of its description and imagery.

a Which of the four short poems in this group makes you 'see and hear' most vividly? How does Browning achieve this?

b Which other poems, or parts of poems, would you choose if you wanted to convince Browning that he had succeeded in making you 'see and hear' the subjects of his poetry?

Home-Thoughts, from Abroad

I

Oh, to be in England
Now that April's there,
And whoever wakes in England
Sees, some morning, unaware,
That the lowest boughs and the brushwood sheaf   5
Round the elm-tree bole are in tiny leaf,
While the chaffinch sings on the orchard bough
In England – now!

II

And after April, when May follows,
And the whitethroat builds, and all the swallows!   10
Hark, where my blossomed pear-tree in the hedge
Leans to the field and scatters on the clover
Blossoms and dewdrops – at the bent spray's edge –
That's the wise thrush; he sings each song twice over,
Lest you should think he never could recapture   15
The first fine careless rapture!
And though the fields look rough with hoary dew,
All will be gay when noontide wakes anew
The buttercups, the little children's dower
– Far brighter than this gaudy melon-flower!   20

'De Gustibus – '

I

Your ghost will walk, you lover of trees,
   (If our loves remain)
   In an English lane,
By a cornfield-side a-flutter with poppies.
Hark, those two in the hazel coppice –   5
A boy and a girl, if the good fates please,
   Making love, say, –
   The happier they!
Draw yourself up from the light of the moon,
And let them pass, as they will too soon,   10
   With the bean-flowers' boon,
   And the blackbird's tune,
   And May, and June!

II

What I love best in all the world
Is a castle, precipice-encurled,   15
In a gash of the wind-grieved Apennine.°
Or look for me, old fellow of mine,
(If I get my head from out the mouth
O' the grave, and loose my spirit's bands,
And come again to the land of lands) –   20
In a sea-side house to the farther South,
Where the baked cicala° dies of drouth,°
And one sharp tree – 'tis a cypress – stands,
By the many hundred years red-rusted,
Rough iron-spiked, ripe fruit-o'ercrusted,   25
My sentinel to guard the sands
To the water's edge. For, what expands
Before the house, but the great opaque
Blue breadth of sea without a break?
While, in the house, for ever crumbles   30
Some fragment of the frescoed walls,

From blisters where a scorpion sprawls.
A girl bare-footed brings, and tumbles
Down on the pavement, green-flesh melons,
And says there's news to-day – the king°   35
Was shot at, touched in the liver-wing,°
Goes with his Bourbon arm in a sling:
– She hopes they have not caught the felons.°
Italy, my Italy!
Queen Mary's° saying serves for me –   40
   (When fortune's malice
    Lost her – Calais) –
Open my heart and you will see
Graved inside of it, 'Italy.'
Such lovers old are I and she: 45
So it always was, so shall ever be!

RESOURCE NOTES

Who has written these poems and why?

Alfred, Lord Tennyson

Alfred Tennyson was born in Lincolnshire in 1809, the fourth in a family of eight sons and four daughters. His father was a country clergyman, who was embittered by having been disinherited by his own father in favour of his younger brother. As a result, he became increasingly susceptible to attacks of physical and mental illness, which made him violent and irrational, and this inevitably affected his own children and his marriage. Throughout his own long life, Tennyson suffered from periods of depression and anxiety about his own health, and he attributed these to a great extent to 'the black blood' of the Tennyson family.

The main events of Tennyson's life are not particularly dramatic, unlike those of Elizabeth Barrett and Robert Browning. He attended Cambridge University, where he met Arthur Hallam, the friend to whom *In Memoriam* is dedicated, left without taking a degree, got engaged to Emily Sellwood, broke off the engagement because of parental opposition to his lack of money, but eventually married her eight years later, in 1850. In the same year, he was made Poet Laureate on the death of William Wordsworth, and in 1883 he was made a peer by Queen Victoria. In his letter to her accepting this honour, he modestly referred to it as:

> a public mark of your majesty's esteem which
> recognises in my person the power of literature in
> this age of the world

but it was also public recognition of the personal status and reputation which Tennyson had achieved. As Poet Laureate he was the national poet, admired and widely read by his contemporaries. He died in 1892, and is buried in Westminster Abbey.

This summary of his life gives little indication of the reasons for Tennyson's reputation as a major Victorian poet. If you look at the Time Line on pages 156–159, it is easier to see the evidence of his single-minded dedication to writing poetry from the record of his publications. For further reasons, you will have to search in the poems themselves, looking at the ways in which Tennyson draws on his own habits of introspection, his own feelings and emotions, particularly about death and bereavement, his personal questions about faith and religion, and his reflections on human behaviour, and the language and forms in which he chooses to express these.

✦ *Activity*

Why do you think Tennyson was a popular poet? As you read his poems, make a note of any aspects of Tennyson's work which you think would have appealed to his Victorian readers. Aim to give a reason for each point, based on your reading of Victorian poetry so far, and add your personal opinions, positive or negative, with your reasons for responding to Tennyson as you do.

Elizabeth Barrett Browning

Elizabeth Barrett was born in 1806, the eldest of twelve children of a middle-class family. Like Tennyson and Browning, she was determined to be a writer – she began her first poem, 'The Battle of Marathon', written 'in the style of Homer, Pope and Byron', when she was eleven. She suffered greatly from ill health, intensified in 1840 by a breakdown following the death by drowning of her favourite brother, Edward. Between 1821 and 1846 she was an invalid, but despite being housebound and often bedridden she continued to write and publish poetry, and to read widely.

In 1844 her complimentary reference to Robert Browning's work, in her poem 'Lady Geraldine's Courtship', encouraged him to write to her, expressing his admiration for her poetry. Their relationship developed through letters and visits by Browning to the Barretts' house in London. It was concealed from her dominating father, who was fiercely protective of Elizabeth, and opposed to the idea of his children marrying unless he entirely approved of their choice of partner. In September 1846 Elizabeth Barrett and Robert Browning were secretly married.

A week after their marriage they left England secretly for Italy. In 1849 their only son, Robert, affectionately known as Pen, was born. From 1846 to 1861, when Elizabeth Barrett Browning died, they lived in Florence, sometimes travelling in Europe, and making short visits to England. Although she tried hard to make contact with her father after her marriage, he refused to forgive her, left her letters unopened, and they were never reconciled. She died in 1861, and is buried in the English cemetery in Florence.

During her lifetime, Elizabeth Barrett Browning was more popular with readers of poetry than her husband, and sold a great deal better than he did. She was suggested as a possible Poet Laureate, alongside Tennyson. Yet while Tennyson and Browning have always been recognised as major representatives of 'English literature', Elizabeth Barrett Browning is more often referred to as a minor Victorian poet, better known for her romantic life story, her love poems, and for being Mrs Robert Browning.

✦ *Activity*

As you read the poems, think about the similarities and differences between the work of these three poets. Do you think the men's poetry is better, or more worth studying, than Elizabeth Barrett Browning's? If so, in what ways do you think it is better? If you do not agree that it is, discuss why not. What reasons can you think of for the differences in the status of the three poets since their deaths?

Robert Browning

Robert Browning was born in 1812. His father was a clerk in the Bank of England, a man with an active interest in art and literature. Browning went to London University, but (like Tennyson) left without taking a degree. Also like Tennyson, Browning decided against a conventional career and determined to devote himself to writing. As a young man he travelled widely, supported financially by his family, who paid for his early work to be published.

Initially Browning was interested in the theatre, and made several unsuccessful attempts at writing for the stage. His early poetry was equally unsuccessful with the reading public – very few copies sold, and reviewers criticised him for being deliberately difficult and obscure. However, he continued to work at his 'novel dramatic method of presenting any phenomenon of the mind or passions', developing the dramatic monologue – the genre of poetry for which he is best known. The titles of some of his collections of poems: *Dramatic Lyrics*, *Dramatic Romances*, *Men and Women*, and *Dramatic Idyls*, emphasise his continuing interest in drama and creating characters. Although he was not generally popular, he had readers who admired his work, one of whom was Elizabeth Barrett Browning. Their courtship, secret marriage and flight to Italy have all the elements of a romantic fairy tale – 'passionate lovers, in curls and side whiskers, oppressed, defiant, eloping', as Virginia Woolf described them in her essay on *Aurora Leigh* (1932) – and this tends to obscure the fact that their relationship grew out of, and continued to be based on, mutual admiration of each other's work as poets.

As well as his reputation for being difficult to understand, Browning has also been labelled a rather shallow optimist – a reputation partly gained by lines such as:

> God's in his heaven; all's right with the world
> (Pippa Passes, 1841)

> Grow old along with me!
> The best is yet to be
> (Rabbi Ben Ezra, 1864)

> One who never turned his back but marched breast
>   forward
> Never doubted clouds would break.
> (Epilogue to Asolando, 1889)

However, the first two quotations are lines spoken by two of his characters, and not by Browning himself, and the first of them is certainly ironic, since Pippa is speaking outside a house where two lovers are quarrelling about the murder of the woman's husband! Alongside these apparently optimistic statements, Browning was acutely affected by adverse criticism of his work. In a letter to Elizabeth Barrett, written before their marriage, he also said of himself:

> For every speck of Vesuvius or Stromboli in my
> microcosm there are huge layers of ice and pits of
> black cold water.

As you read his poems, watch out for evidence of volcanic energy, and also of a darker side to his view of life.

Browning's reputation as a poet developed differently from either Tennyson's or his wife's. While Tennyson's seems to have grown fairly steadily, and Elizabeth Barrett Browning's flourished while she was alive, Browning's popularity with readers came late in his life, after his wife's death; eventually he was recognised by his contemporaries as a great dramatic poet. He died in Venice in 1889, shortly after receiving a telegram telling him that his latest poem had been well reviewed. He is buried in Westminster Abbey.

✦ *Activity*

As you read the poems, keep a reading journal and make a note of the poems which you, as a modern reader, find most interesting. Which of the poets do you prefer? Is this because of their subject matter, or their style of writing, or does knowing something about their life story influence you?

If you want to know more about the Brownings' lives, read the biography of Elizabeth Barrett Browning, *Lady's Maid*, by the novelist Margaret Forster. It is a fictionalised biography of Elizabeth Barrett's maid, Wilson, who accompanied the couple to Italy.

Why did they write these poems?

The broad but simple answer to this question is that all three writers had a strong sense of themselves as poets. Even though they all create characters and tell stories, they chose not to be novelists; even though their poetry has elements of drama in it and both Tennyson and Browning made several (unsuccessful) attempts to write plays, they chose not to be playwrights. They all chose to be poets.

Poets do not have a significant role in society today – for moral, social and political comment there are journalists, commentators and 'experts', television and film, documentaries, fiction and drama. But the Victorians had a strong sense of what the role of a poet ought to be. Poetry to the Victorians was a superior kind of writing with a long history, reaching back to Greek and Latin literature. They tended to think of novels as inferior, popular forms of writing, and as for drama in England, for most of the nineteenth century it was either versions of Shakespeare or melodramas and popular spectacles. The Victorians felt that a poet ought to teach his or her readers in some way, as well as giving them the aesthetic pleasure that comes from reading beautifully expressed emotions, descriptions or ideas. Tennyson and the Brownings understood this role. As you can see from the variety of different kinds of poem which they wrote, they also understood that writing poetry is a craft, with its own techniques and disciplines, and that a poet has to be technically skilled.

✦ *Activity*

In groups, interview each of the 'poets' in turn. Ask each 'poet':
- what he or she thinks their strengths as a poet are
- what kind of poetry they like writing best
- what subject matter appeals to them most
- what opportunities they think different subjects have offered them, as poets
- what messages they want to convey to their readers.

The answers given by the 'poets' must be based on the evidence of the poems you have read.

For example, Tennyson might reply, 'When I was a young man I loved to write descriptions … I chose stories like … But later on …'

Elizabeth Barrett Browning might begin, 'As a woman, I feel especially drawn to … but … '

and Robert Browning would probably start off 'People … that's what interests me … '

Dates	Tennyson	Elizabeth Barrett Browning	Robert Browning	Some key events and publications
1806		Born near Durham		
1809	Born in Lincolnshire			
1812			Born in South London	
1815				End of Napoleonic Wars
1819		*The Battle of Marathon* privately published		Birth of Queen Victoria; Peterloo Massacre
1832	'Mariana'; 'The Sleeping Beauty'; 'The Lady of Shalott'			Parliamentary Reform Bill
1833	Death of Arthur Hallam			
1834	'Break, Break, Break'; 'Ulysses'; 'Morte d'Arthur' and some sections of *In Memoriam* (not published for 17 years)			Tolpuddle Martyrs

Year				
1837				Queen Victoria begins her reign
1838			Family move to Wimpole St, London	Chartist movement
1840		'Sordello'	Death of brother; breakdown	Economic depression: the 'hungry 40s'
1841		'Pippa Passes'		
1842		'Dramatic Lyrics' 'My Last Duchess'		Report: *Children's Employment Commission*
1843			'The Cry of the Children'	
1844				Factory Act
1845		'Bishop Orders his Tomb…', 'The Laboratory', 1st letter to EBB		
1846			EBB and RB marry. They leave England for Italy	
1847	*The Princess*		'Runaway Slave at Pilgrim's Point'	Charlotte Brontë *Jane Eyre*; Emily Brontë *Wuthering Heights*; William Makepeace Thackeray *Vanity Fair*

Dates	Tennyson	Elizabeth Barrett Browning	Robert Browning	Some key events and publications
1848				Year of revolutions in Europe; Communist Manifesto; Mrs Gaskell *Mary Barton*
1849		Birth of son, Robert (nicknamed Pen)		
1850	*In Memoriam* Appointed Poet Laureate	'Sonnets from the Portuguese' 'Flush or Faunus'		William Wordsworth dies
1851				Mayhew: *London Labour and the London Poor*
1853				Charles Dickens *Bleak House*
1854				Charles Dickens *Hard Times*
1855	*Maud*		*Men and Women*: 'Fra Lippo Lippi' 'Childe Roland' 'Andrea del Sarto'	Crimean War begins
1856		*Aurora Leigh*		Crimean War ends
1857				Indian Mutiny

Year				
1859				Charles Darwin: *On The Origin of Species*
1860				England supports Italian unification
1861		Died in Florence, Italy		Death of Prince Albert; Charles Dickens *Great Expectations*
1863			Poetical works re-published in 3 volumes	
1869	*Idylls of the King* (including 'Morte d'Arthur' 1832)			
1872				George Eliot *Middlemarch*
1876				Queen Victoria becomes Empress of India
1884	Made an hereditary peer			
1887				Queen Victoria's Golden Jubilee
1889	'Crossing the Bar'	Died in Venice, Italy		
1892	Died in Surrey			
1901				Death of Queen Victoria

What type of texts are these poems?

You probably feel confident that you can recognise a poem when you see one, but how exactly do you define poetry (see page 8)? Under the umbrella of 'poetry', as distinct from 'prose' or 'drama', lies a huge variety of different types of poem which poets can choose from as a vehicle for their ideas. Modern readers tend to think of poetry almost exclusively as lyric poetry and therefore expect poems to be fairly short, condensed expressions of personal thoughts and feelings. The Victorian poets and their readers were familiar with a much wider range of poetry and of poetic forms, which included the lyric as one kind of poem among many.

In this collection, as well as reading poems about love and death and personal feelings, you can also read poetry which tells stories (as novels do), creates characters in action (as drama does), evokes places, atmospheres and moods (as film can do) and criticises the way things are in society (as political speeches do). You can read ballads, blank verse, elegies, epics, lyrics, narratives, dramatic monologues, songs and sonnets. You will recognise all of them as poetry, even though they cross the boundaries of the genres into the usual territories of prose or drama at times.

One striking difference between Victorian and much modern poetry is in the poets' handling of form and use of poetic techniques: rhyme, rhythm, the uses of figurative language – similes and metaphors – and the poets' choices of language to create effects and describe situations, settings and emotions. The discipline involved in writing formal verse, with a set rhyme scheme, a regular rhythm and a repeated pattern for each stanza is much more noticeable than it is in much modern poetry written in free verse, with its different, less obvious rules.

✦ *Activities*

1a In groups, look up in a dictionary and discuss your definitions of the following types of poem:
- ballad
- blank verse

- elegy
- epic
- narrative
- dramatic monologue
- song
- sonnet

Find examples of these in the collection.

b   Draw up a grid of the different kinds of poems to be found in this collection, e.g narrative poems, lyrics and songs, personal poems, poems about issues (women's rights, slavery, child labour), dramatic monologues, explorations of psychology etc. Sort out the poems under the headings. You can put the same poem in several different places. Then compare your grid with a partner's.

c   Look at how the poems are written, and the forms the poets have chosen, as well as at their subject matter. Use your grid as the basis for comparing the ways in which the different poets write a similar type of poem. For each category, you could add a modern poem of the same type to compare with the nineteenth-century ones.

2 The sources for some of the poems are printed with them:
- William Shakespeare's *Measure for Measure* ('Mariana') page 13
- Sir Thomas Malory ('Morte d'Arthur') page 27
- the Evidence from the Children's Commission ('Cry of the Children') pages 76–77
- Georgio Vasari's *Lives of the Artists* ('Frà Lippo Lippi' and 'Andrea del Sarto') pages 117–119.

Compare the source with the relevant poem:

a What has been added in reworking it into a poem? (Remember to think about forms and choices of language as well as content when you discuss this.)

b Which version do you prefer and why?

c What do you think has been gained or lost in the reworking?

How were these poems produced?

Alfred, Lord Tennyson and Robert Browning had very different methods of writing. Tennyson revised his work obsessively. For him reviewing and revising were literally processes of re-seeing his poems. According to his descendant, Sir Charles Tennyson, he had a habit of 'borrowing' from himself:

> He stored observations and similes for long periods
> before finally working them into his poems.

Something he had written years before would eventually be found a place in a later, longer work. For example, *Maud* grew out of a lyric which begins:

> O that 'twere possible
> After long grief and pain
> To find the arms of my true love
> Round me once again.

This now appears in the middle of Part II of the monodrama. Of the creation of *In Memoriam*, Tennyson said:

> The sections were written at many different places,
> and as the phases of our intercourse came to my
> memory and suggested them. I did not write them
> with any view of weaving them into a whole, or for
> publication, until I found I had written so many.
> (Hallam Tennyson, *Alfred, Lord Tennyson: a
> Memoir*, 1897)

Robert Browning wrote much more rapidly, and was unsympathetic to Tennyson's painstaking methods. He said of *Poems, 1842*:

> Whatever is touched is spoiled. There is some
> woeful mental infirmity in the man – he was months
> buried in correcting the press of the last volume,

and in that time began spoiling the new poems ... as
hard as he could.

(Letters, 1842)

Perhaps this says more about Browning's temperament than it
does about the quality of Tennyson's poems, but Browning
certainly disliked the physical act of writing. In March 1845 he
wrote to Elizabeth Barrett, who, herself, was a prolific letter
writer as well as a committed poet:

> I have no pleasure in writing myself – none, in the
> mere act ... my heart sinks whenever I open this
> desk, and rises when I shut it.

Partly because of this, and partly because he found it easier to
revise his work if he could see it printed or written in a different
handwriting from his own, he used to get his sister to copy his
poems out for him. He did then correct his work, but not as
intensively as Tennyson did. During their courtship, he and
Elizabeth Barrett developed the habit of exchanging poems and
comments on them; when he was preparing the first volume of his
poetry to be published after their marriage, he asked his wife for
advice and criticism. She admired his work greatly, but like other
readers she found some of it 'obscure, elliptical and difficult',
faults which she had been accused of herself. Many of her
suggested alterations were intended to clarify meaning, or to
smooth out what she thought were roughnesses in the verse. The
effect was to interfere with Browning's characteristic poetic style
and he eventually came to distrust the whole process of revising.
In later volumes, published after her death, Robert Browning
returned to the original versions of the poems.

The conditions which they preferred for writing were also
different. Tennyson worked regularly every day, whereas Robert
Browning generally worked more irregularly and spasmodically.
However, there were times during his marriage to Elizabeth,
while he was writing *Men and Women* and she was writing
Aurora Leigh, when they established a productive routine,
working similar hours each day, but in separate rooms, not

showing each other their as yet unfinished work. Elizabeth Barrett Browning's view was that:

> an artist must ... either find or make a solitude to
> work in, if it is to be good work at all.
>> (Letter to Henry Chorley, 1851)

Use of sources

Traditionally, readers of poetry have had a rather romantic idea of the importance of 'inspiration' to a poet, and put a high premium on originality of ideas and choice of subject. Poetry written 'to order' – as England's Poet Laureate is still expected to do on occasions of national importance such as royal births, marriages, anniversaries and deaths – is often considered inferior to the work the same writer produces independently.

The Victorians saw the role of the poet and the function of poetry differently. The poets were conscious of their responsibility to 'teach' as well as to entertain their readers, and in return they were given respect and status in their society. Tennyson found ideas for many of his poems in his reading of the classics, and English legends and history. He also welcomed suggestions for subjects on which he could base poems – in fact, he invited them. Elizabeth Barrett Browning used earlier poets as models, but also responded to requests for poems which would support campaigns and raise political issues. Robert Browning had strong views about independence and originality. In answer to a question about the historical origin of one of his characters, he wrote:

> poetry, if it is to deserve the name, ought to create –
> or re-animate something – not merely reproduce
> raw fact taken from somebody else's book.
>> (Letter to Mrs Fitzgerald, March 1883)

But he too found subjects in his reading, especially about art and history. One of his last major works, *The Ring and the Book*, a novel-length series of interlocking monologues all telling the same dramatic story set in seventeenth-century Italy, was inspired by his discovery of a bundle of old documents on a market stall in Florence. In all three cases, the poets' originality lies in their different approaches to, and treatment of their sources, and their skill in reworking them for their contemporary readers.

✦ *Activity*

Information about a writer's methods of working comes from published conversations, letters, diaries, journals and memoirs, as well as their manuscripts. There is also evidence that Robert Browning used to produce first drafts of at least some of his poems in prose.

Choose one of the poems, and put yourself in the role of its author. In a letter, a diary entry, a prose draft, or a conversation with an interested friend, explain how you planned the poem, the effects you wanted to achieve and the ideas which you hoped to convey to the reader.

―――――――――――――――― ✦ ――――――――――――――――

How do these poets present their subjects?

This section is intended to help you to think more about the similarities and differences between the work of these three poets. In terms of subject matter and themes they have a good deal in common:

- telling stories, old and new
- studying people, their behaviour and emotions
- exploring themes of love and death, belief and doubt, definitions of femininity and masculinity, and issues in society.

Alfred, Lord Tennyson, Elizabeth Barrett Browning and Robert Browning also have a good deal in common in the ways they use language. They draw on a fund of references to the Bible, and to myths and legends. They often refer to literature written before the nineteenth century, which their readers would probably also have known well, but which may be much less familiar to readers today. When recreating scenes and stories from the past, they use strange, archaic words which would have been unfamiliar even to their contemporaries. They commit themselves to the disciplines of writing many different kinds of formal verse, and often compress or twist their sentences, or the usual order of the words, to meet the constraints of rhythm and rhyme. All three write long poems, full of sharply observed descriptive details.

But despite so many similarities, each of the poets has what Tennyson's friend, Arthur Hallam, called 'distinctive excellencies'.

In 1831, Hallam wrote an essay 'On some of the characteristics of modern poetry, and on the lyrical poems of Alfred Tennyson'. In this he summed up the five features of Tennyson's work which he thought made him a significant poet, even so early in his career. In Hallam's own words, these were:

- his luxuriance of imagination, and his control over it
- his power of embodying himself in ideal characters, and their moods
- his vivid, picturesque delineation of objects, and the skill with which he fuses them with emotion

166

- the variety of his lyrical measures
- the elevated habits of thought in these compositions.

This list was written before Tennyson had published most of the poems in this selection, but it gives a good idea of what one of his contemporaries looked for and admired in a poet.

✦ *Activity*

a In a group, discuss the meaning of each statement in turn and find examples from Tennyson's poems which you think illustrate it. For example, by 'lyrical measures', Hallam means the different kinds of verse forms Tennyson uses.

b As a modern reader, how far do you agree with Hallam's praise of each of these features of Tennyson's work?

Elizabeth Barrett Browning and Robert Browning

Early in 1845, shortly after they had met for the first time, Robert Browning wrote to Elizabeth Barrett:

> Your poetry ... must be infinitely more to me than
> mine to you – for you do what I always wanted,
> hoped to do ... You speak out, you – I only make
> men and women speak – give you truth broken into
> prismatic lines, and fear the pure white light, even if
> it is in me ...
>
> (Letter, 13 January 1845)

Robert Browning identifies what he thinks is the fundamental difference between their work: that she writes personally and in her own voice, while he can only impersonate the voices of other people.

✦ *Activities*

1 Which poem, or poems, would you choose as examples of Browning's description of his wife's work? Do you think he is fair to himself in this comparison between them?

2 With a partner, make lists similar to Hallam's of the special qualities of the poems of Elizabeth Barrett Browning and Robert Browning.

Architecture, art and poetry

All artists react to the past in some way. Some rebel against it; others draw on it to adapt and reinvent subjects and styles. If you did some preliminary research before you began to read these poems, you may have noticed some connections between the poetry and the visual arts of the period. Victorian architects built in styles taken from all over the world, and from any historical period. They created banks and museums, public buildings and railway stations that look like Greek temples, fairy palaces or castles from medieval paintings. They embellished these buildings with decorative motifs, sometimes drawn from nature, sometimes from the arts of different parts of the British Empire, sometimes from classical models.

Close links between literature and the visual arts can be seen in the work of the painters who called themselves the Pre-Raphaelite Brotherhood (1848–1860s). The most important founder members of this group were John Everett Millais, Dante Gabriel Rossetti and William Holman Hunt, followed later by Edward Burne Jones and John William Waterhouse. They were inspired by literary, historical and religious subjects, and wanted to return to the kind of painting they found in fifteenth-century Italian art, before Raphael (1483–1520) had become a major influence. Many of their paintings are based on the same subjects as those chosen by poets: classical myths and legends, the Bible, stories of King Arthur and his knights. Many illustrate poems ('The Lady of Shalott' was a particularly popular subject) or scenes from William Shakespeare's plays. As well as similarities of subject matter, there are also similarities in the painters' and poets' uses of images. Poems and paintings are full of flowers and fruit, birds and animals, often used symbolically as well as realistically.

Approaches to narrative

The Victorians loved stories, in poetry and paintings, as well as in prose. As well as the two-way traffic between the Pre-Raphaelites and poets, Victorian artists also painted scenes of contemporary life which drew attention to social conditions and issues in ways perhaps more similar to those of nineteenth-century novelists. These pictures have titles like: 'The Awakening Conscience', 'The Last Day in the Old Home', 'The Emigrant's Last Sight of Home', 'Thoughts of the Past', 'A Hopeless Dream' and 'Woman's Mission: Companion of Manhood'. The paintings convey strong narratives through their portrayals of character and situation. Visual details which also have symbolic significance are deliberately chosen as essential elements in the story the picture tells. Victorian poetry and paintings also share similar attitudes to central concerns of the age, especially the roles of women. The Middle Ages – or a romanticised nineteenth-century interpretation of them – seem to have appealed especially to Victorian poets and artists because that period provided wonderful stories. These stories, as well as giving ample scope for the inventive use of decorative details in words or visual images, could also be reinterpreted to reinforce nineteenth-century views of femininity and masculinity, and the relationships between the sexes.

✦ *Activities*

1 Find a Victorian narrative picture, and look carefully at it. With a partner, compare the stories the picture suggests to you.

2 If you made a grid of different types of poem (see page 161), remind yourself of how many of the poems tell a story. The three poets differ in the ways they choose to use stories, and handle narrative. Here are some of the ways: can you attach titles of poems to each item on this list, and add to it? Stories are told:
   • directly and chronologically
   • indirectly: the story emerges as the poem proceeds
   • to recreate the past
   • as an opportunity to create mood and atmosphere
   • as an opportunity to explore psychology
   • through a first person narrative
   • through a third person narrative.

Voice

When reading poems it is always helpful to ask yourself the question, 'Who is "speaking" here? Is it the poet himself or herself, or a character the poet has created?' A poem is not necessarily autobiographical – it may equally well be an attempt to explore ideas and feelings that readers recognise and share. Tennyson gives a valuable warning about making assumptions about a poet's use of 'I' in his comments about his writing of *In Memoriam*:

> The different moods of sorrow as in a drama are
> dramatically given, and my conviction that fear,
> doubts and suffering will find answer and relief only
> through faith in a God of Love. 'I' is not always the
> author speaking of himself, but the voice of the
> human race speaking through him.
>
> (Hallam Tennyson, *Alfred, Lord Tennyson: a*
> *Memoir*, 1897)

✦ *Activity*

All three poets use a variety of distinctive voices, their own and other people's. Make a grid with three columns, one for each poet, and list the different speakers you find in the poems. Include the poet himself or herself, and omniscient narrators, as well as named characters.

The dramatic monologue

Robert Browning is the master of the dramatic monologue, but Tennyson and Elizabeth Barrett Browning also often used this poetic form, and it continues to be popular and much used by poets today. The 'rules', or literary conventions, of the dramatic monologue are:

- a single speaker, whose character and personality are revealed through their speech
- a silent listener
- a situation which emerges as the poem proceeds, rather than being stated directly
- the poem begins in the middle of the 'action'.

It is closest to a soliloquy or an aside in a play, but differs from these, because the conventions of the 'aside' are that it is a short remark to the audience which other characters on the stage do not overhear – it may or may not reveal character. In William Shakespeare's plays at least, a character who speaks a soliloquy is alone on the stage and addresses the audience directly, speaking truthfully about themselves, whatever impression they may have given to other characters in the play. In the dramatic monologue, the character speaks. It is up to the reader to decide whether or not the character realises how much truth about themselves they are revealing.

Reading aloud

Many of the poems are so dramatic in their effects that they ask to be performed aloud, despite their length. Tennyson always insisted that *Maud* was a performance poem, and he often read his work aloud to friends, as did Robert Browning. It is still possible to hear a very old recording of Tennyson reading 'The Charge of the Light Brigade' – and to imagine from the way he intones that poem what his reading of *Maud* must have sounded like.

Preparing a poem to present to an audience is a good way of focusing closely on meaning and effect. It will also help you to experience the way in which Robert Browning is especially skilful in the way he uses appropriate rhythms of ordinary speech as one of his techniques of creating character.

◆ *Activities*

1 In a small group read aloud to each other 'Ulysses' and the extracts from either 'Frà Lippo Lippi' or 'Andrea del Sarto'. All these poems are written in blank verse – unrhyming ten-syllable lines (pentameters), with five strong stresses to a line (iambics) – the verse form often used by Shakespeare in his plays.
   a Which poem sounds most like normal speech?
   b How does the poem achieve this effect?

2 Choose a poem and annotate it with instructions for reading it aloud. Mark:
   - pauses
   - changes of pace, and the reason for them
   - changes of mood
   - changes of tone and volume.

3 Choose two of the dramatic monologues, each by a different poet. Compare the different ways in which the character of the speaker is created, focusing particularly on how he or she talks: choices of vocabulary, tricks of speech, tone and pace, lengths of sentences, pauses etc.

4 Analyse the characters and settings of Browning's dramatic monologues, using these headings:
   - title
   - main character
   - their characteristics
   - the setting
   - other characters in the poem.

   Choose one of the poems, and use it to write your own dramatic monologue, from the point of view of one of the silent characters in it. Try to imitate the form and style of the original as closely as you can.

5 In a small group, choose one of the dramatic monologues in *Three Victorian Poets* to present to the rest of the class. To do this you might:
   a use the poem as the basis for an improvised version of it, in which the silent listeners also speak
   b have one person reading the monologue while the others interrupt with their reactions to, and comments about, what is being said
   c in groups, imagine you are some of the other people also mentioned in the monologue, and in those roles discuss what you have just seen and heard. For example:

- the Count's servant reports to his master ('My Last Duchess')
- the Bishop's 'nephews' discuss his dying wishes ('The Bishop Orders his Tomb at Saint Praxed's Church')
- Ulysses' wife and his son talk about his plans for a final journey ('Ulysses')
- the jury decide their verdict on the runaway slave ('The Runaway Slave at Pilgrim's Point').

◆

Who reads these poems?
How do they interpret them?

Poetry is just as susceptible to changes in public taste and fashion as any other part of people's lives. During their lifetimes all three poets were recognised as significant literary figures; now they are probably not much read except as part of literature courses in schools and universities. Victorian readers made their enthusiasm for *Aurora Leigh* clear by buying up twelve editions between 1856 and 1900, and by making *In Memoriam* the most widely read and most appreciated poem of the age about death and bereavement. Prince Albert was a great admirer of *In Memoriam* and Queen Victoria found the lyric 'Be near me when my light is low' especially comforting after his death in 1861. *In Memoriam* must have contributed a great deal to Tennyson's status as the national poet at a time when everyone had to face the likelihood of the early death of close members of their family, or friends. Robert Browning was much less popular during his lifetime, and his work continues to challenge modern readers. However, his poems may be more accessible now than Tennyson's lengthy narrative poems, luxuriant, musical descriptions and personal feelings about religious faith and doubt.

Early critics

Critics in the nineteenth century seem to have been much more insulting, and often more humorous or witty, than they are today, and so it is not surprising that all three poets were extremely sensitive to adverse criticism. One reviewer said of 'The Lady of Shalott' that it was:

> an onion which could make nobody shed tears.

Maud, the first poem Tennyson published after becoming Poet Laureate, was very unfavourably received. Readers must have found the content and emotions in this poem a shock from the author of *In Memoriam*. So how do you suppose Tennyson felt about one critic's comment, that if either of the vowels in the title were omitted, all that needed to be said about the poem would be revealed?

Elizabeth Barrett Browning said that when *Aurora Leigh* was published she 'expected to be put in the stocks as a disorderly woman and free thinking poet'. The reviews were not universally complimentary – one critic said that in this work she was 'often more coarsely masculine than any other woman writer'. (Note how the statement reveals some interesting assumptions on this person's part about how women were expected to write in 1856.) However, others praised her for the way she dealt with 'modern life and issues', and the first edition sold out in a fortnight.

From the start Robert Browning was criticised by his contemporaries for his obscurity. Jane Carlyle, the wife of the Victorian historian and thinker, Thomas Carlyle, knew Tennyson and the Brownings. She claimed to have read Robert Browning's early poem, 'Sordello', but still did not know whether Sordello was a man, a city or a book. Tennyson, who recognised and respected Browning as a fellow poet, said he had understood only two lines in it – the first and the last. On the day of publication in 1855, a contemporary reviewer of Robert Browning's *Men and Women* wrote:

> Who will not grieve over energy wasted and power
> misspent, – over fancies chaste and noble, so
> overhung by the 'seven veils' of obscurity … ?
> *(The Athenaeum*, 17 November 1855)

Ways of reading

Even readers who want to be positive about a writer can have problems with some of their work. John Ruskin (1819–1900), the art historian and critic, wrote Browning a long letter in December 1855, about *Men and Women*. In it he explains, as politely as he can, the difficulties he has in reading the poems:

> Of their power there can of course be no question
> … but … being hard worked at present, and not
> able to give the cream of the day to poetry – when I
> take up these poems in the evening I find them

absolutely and literally a set of the most amazing
Conundrums that ever were proposed to me. I try at
them for – say twenty minutes – in which time I
make out about twenty lines, always having to miss
two, for every one I make out. I enjoy the twenty,
each separately very much, but the puzzlement
about the intermediate ones increases in
comfortlessness till I get a headache, and give in.

The rest of his letter submits one of the poems to an intensive interrogation, in which he questions statements made in it, takes things literally, criticises Browning's grammar and sentence structure, and picks holes in his choice of words and his use of rhythm. He compares the effort of reading the poems to mountaineering:

You are worse than the worst Alpine Glacier I ever
crossed. Bright and deep enough truly, but so full of
clefts that half the journey has to be done with a
ladder and hatchet.

(Ruskin to Browning, Letter: London,
2 December 1855)

The tone of Browning's reply (below) is equally friendly, but he focuses on the differences in the ways in which he and Ruskin read poetry. Browning obviously expects an active reader, who will collaborate with him in the effort to make meaning from his writing – a very twentieth-century view of what readers do when they read.

We don't read poetry the same way, by the same
law; it is too clear. I cannot begin writing poetry
until my imaginary reader has conceded licences to
me which you demur at altogether ... You would
have me paint it all plain out, which can't be; but by
various artifices I try to make shift with touches and
bits and outlines which succeed if they bear the
conception from me to you. You ought, I think, to

keep pace with the thought tripping from ledge to
ledge of my 'glaciers', as you call them; not stand
poking your alpenstock into the holes, and
demonstrating that no foot could have stood there.
Suppose it sprang over there? In prose you may
criticise so but ...

> (Browning to Ruskin, Letter: Paris,
> 10 December 1855)

Twentieth-century critics

Most writers' reputations decline after their deaths, and then may
or may not be re-established. The power to maintain a writer's
reputation or allow it to slip into obscurity rests mainly in the
hands of critics, publishers and, in the case of poetry, editors of
anthologies. The critic largely responsible for the lack of interest
in Victorian poetry during much of the twentieth century was F.
R. Leavis, who taught at Cambridge between 1959 and his death
in 1978. He had a great and lasting influence in shaping the way
many readers respond to literature, and he disliked almost
everything about Tennyson and Robert Browning, especially the
poets' styles and their subject matter. He accused
nineteenth-century poetry of being 'characteristically
preoccupied with the creation of a dream world'. T. S. Eliot
(1888–1965), the poet and critic, whom Leavis did admire, was
more generous, especially to Tennyson. In his essay on *In
Memoriam* he praises some of the same qualities as Arthur
Hallam had done almost 100 years earlier, especially his technical
accomplishment, and his 'unique and unerring feeling for the
sound of words'. Although poems by Tennyson and Robert
Browning continue to be recognised as part of England's 'literary
heritage', critics have only fairly recently begun to re-read and
reconsider their work independently.

After 1900 Elizabeth Barrett Browning virtually disappeared
as a writer, although she lived on in literary biography as the
heroine of a fairy story, imprisoned by her cruel father, rescued by
Robert Browning, the handsome prince, and reborn as a wife and
mother. *Aurora Leigh* went out of print and therefore remained
unread, despite Virginia Woolf's attempt to revive it in 1932 in

her essay in *The Second Common Reader*, until the feminist publishing house, Virago, reprinted it in 1978. In the introduction to her biography of the poet, first published in 1988, Margaret Forster writes:

> One of the aims of this biography is to stimulate more interest in Elizabeth Barrett Browning's poetry. This being so, it was a shock to discover that this is largely inaccessible outside a good library.
>
> (*Elizabeth Barrett Browning*, 1988)

Critics can diminish or destroy interest in writers; they can also create and develop it. One of the achievements of feminist criticism since the 1970s has been not only to rediscover the work of women writers like Elizabeth Barrett Browning, but also to go back and look again at earlier assumptions and prejudices about it.

Your reading

It is important to remember that any critics, however prestigious and well educated, are only expressing their personal response to what they have read – you have the same freedom to read and re-read, and to make up your own mind about the text. It would be surprising if you didn't find yourself disagreeing as well as agreeing with their judgements. The following activities are intended to give you an opportunity to consider the poems you have read from different perspectives, and to decide what these Victorian poets have to offer readers today.

✦ *Activities*

1 Find four or five anthologies of English poetry, preferably published since 1900. How are Tennyson, Elizabeth Barrett Browning and Robert Browning represented in them? Do you think the editor of the anthology has a particular personal view of each writer that has guided their choice of poems?

2 Imagine that you have been asked to edit a series of anthologies. Which of the poems from *Three Victorian Poets* would you choose to include in a volume of:
  • 100 great poems
  • 100 readable poems
  • poems to take to a desert island
  • poems for people who dislike poetry.

3 Prepare the case for and against including the work of these three poets in a course of study:
  • for people interested in English literature
  • for people interested in history
  • for school students aged 11–14
  • for English examinations
  • for students for whom English is an additional language.

4 Take any of the statements about the poems and poets quoted from reviewers and critics as the basis for a piece of writing of your own, either arguing against the statement or agreeing with it.

5 Construct Victorian role cards for a group of four or five people: e.g. mother, father, daughter in love, another writer, critic. Draw a card each, and pick a poet. Discuss your reactions to their poems, from the point of view of the Victorian character stated on your card. You could fill in more details about the moral and religious principles of the parents, or the points of view of the writer and the critic, or invent other characters, if you wish.

6 Robert Browning called one of his volumes of poetry *Men and Women*. How do the three poets present men and women to us?
  a Write sets of statements for each of the poets, using this framework: In … [the name of the poem] … [the poet's name] presents the woman as … He / she presents men / the man as …
  b How much do the poets seem to agree and disagree about men and women? How much do you agree with them?

c How are women presented in the Victorian paintings you have looked at? In what ways does this compare with the presentation of women in the poems you have read?

7 Nineteenth-century painters found poetry and literature a rich source of inspiration. Look at some reproductions of Victorian paintings, especially by the Pre-Raphaelites, which are based on a specific text. (For example, you could use the paintings by Holman Hunt, Millais, Rossetti and Waterhouse, all based on 'The Lady of Shalott'.) Discuss the artists' interpretations of the poem, and the ways they and the writer create a sense of time and place, and use visual details.

◆

GLOSSARY

Tennyson

'Mariana'
13   **grange:** country house
       athwart: across
       flats, fen: flat, marshy land
14   **marish:** growing in a marsh
       wainscot: wood panelling
15   **thick-moted:** full of specks of dust

from *The Daydream*
16   **mantles:** cloaks
17   **Oriel:** a large projecting window
       brake: brushwood
19   **cataract:** waterfall

'The Lady of Shalott'
20   **wold:** open country
       shallop: small open boat
21   **stay:** stops weaving
       pad: horse
22   **greaves:** leg armour
       baldric: sash across his shoulder, to hold a bugle or sword

'Morte d'Arthur': Malory's prose version
27   **leve:** loved
       eft: again
       weened: believed
28   **tarried:** delayed

'Morte d'Arthur': Tennyson's poem
29   **unsolders:** breaks apart
       Merlin: (in Arthurian legend) the wizard, Arthur's teacher and guide
       brand: sword
       samite: silk

30   **mere:** lake
       lightly: quickly
       hest: command
       waterflags: flowers like irises
       marge: edge

31   **fëalty:** oath of obedience
       lief: loved
       chased: engraved

35   **casque:** helmet
       greaves and cuisses: leg armour
       onset: blood

36   **Avilion:** (in Arthurian legend) the Isles of the Blest; paradise

'Ulysses'

39   **mete and dole:** give out, administer
       lees: dregs

'Now sleeps the crimson petal'

43   **porphyry:** a reddish purple stone
       Danae: (in Greek mythology) she was visited by the god, Jove (or Jupiter), who made love to her disguised as a shower of gold

'Blame not thyself'

45   **Lethe:** (in Greek mythology) the river of forgetfulness in the Underworld
       burgeon: grow quickly
       thews: muscles

In Memoriam
XXIV

51   **orb:** form into

XXV

51   **cleave:** split
       lading: burden

XXVIII

52   **four changes:** each church has four bells, ringing tunes, or peals, using the bells in different sequences
      Yule: Christmas

LXVII

55   **place of rest:** the church where Hallam is buried

LXXVIII

56   **hoodman-blind:** blind man's buff

CV

57   **within the stranger's land:** Tennyson had moved from the house Hallam had visited when he was alive
      wassail: spiced wine
      mantle: foam

CVII

59   **grides:** rubs together

CXV

60   **quick:** living things (as in 'the quick and the dead')

Maud

Part I

65   **wann'd:** turned pale

67   **musk:** perfume
      in his own behoof: to his own advantage
      hustings: the platform from which he makes his electioneering speeches

68   **gewgaw:** cheap, tasteless, extravagant
      splenetic: bad tempered

Part III

73   **the Black and the Baltic deep:** the Black Sea and the Baltic Sea

'Crossing the Bar'

74   **bar:** sandbank at the mouth of a harbour

Elizabeth Barrett Browning

'The Cry of the Children'
79   **kirk-chime:** church bell
       cerement: shroud; clothes someone is buried in
82   **mart:** market place; crowd

'The Runaway Slave at Pilgrim's Point'
85   **cark:** burden
87   **amulet:** lucky charm
90   **Union:** the union of Northern and Southern states of America
91   **swoon:** faint

Sonnets from the Portuguese
XXVII
95   **asphodel:** (in Greek mythology) an immortal flower which grows in paradise
XXXVIII
95   **meed:** what a person deserves
       chrism: consecrated oil, used in important church ceremonies, like coronations

from Aurora Leigh
Book 1
100   **Bene … che ch'è:** Italian for 'Well', 'What's that?'
       instructed piety: Aurora's aunt gives her all sorts of materials to read about religion, as well as teaching her conventional prayers, the collects and the catechism.
       Balzac: Honoré de Balzac (1799–1850), French novelist
       neologism: new, modern words
       Oviedo: city in Spain
       Chimborazo: mountain in South America
101   **Tophet:** Hell
       Cellarius: a waltz
Book 2
102   **oakum:** fibres unpicked from rope

Book 5

102 **Charlemagne:** hero of the Crusades in the eighth century.
103 **Roland, Roncesvalles:** the most famous of Charlemagne's
knights. He died in a battle against the Saracens, but the
sound of his horn warned Charlemagne and saved his life.

'Flush or Faunus'

105 **Faunus:** a mythological creature, half man, half goat
Arcadian: someone who lives in Arcadia, the country
paradise of Greek mythology
Pan: (in Greek mythology) the god of nature

Robert Browning

'Porphyria's Lover'
108 **dissever:** cut

'My Last Duchess'
110 **Frà:** Friar, brother – a monk artist. (See 'Fra Lippo Lippi', page 117)
favour: gift

'The Bishop Orders his Tomb'
115 **vanity:** futility, pointlessness. The Bishop is quoting from the Bible, Ecclesiastes Ch 1. 'Vanity of vanities, all is vanity, saith the preacher. What profit hath a man of all his labour, which he taketh under the sun?'
cozened: cheated
basalt: black stone
onion-stone: cheap marble
116 **frail:** basket made of rushes
lapis lazuli: blue semi-precious stone
bas-relief: sculpture
thyrsus: (in Greek mythology) the staff carried by the god Dionysus (or Bacchus), god of wine
tables: tablets of stone on which the Ten Commandments were written
travertine: white stone used for ordinary buildings

'Fra Lippo Lippi'
122 **Carmine:** the Carmelites' monastery
Cosimo of the Medici: the ruler of Florence in the fifteenth century
tittle: a tiny detail
123 **mew:** cage
124 **shucks:** husks, pods
125 **the Eight:** the magistrates of Florence
antiphonary: hymn book

Andrea del Sarto

129 **Fiesole:** a small Italian town, near Florence
130 **Morello:** mountain to the north of Florence
131 **Michel Agnolo:** Michelangelo Buonarroti (1475–1564), Florentine sculptor, painter, architect, and poet.
132 **Rafael:** Raphael (Raffaello Santi,1483–1520), Italian painter and architect.
Leonard: Leonardo da Vinci (1452–1519), Italian painter, sculptor, architect, and engineer.

'Childe Roland to the Dark Tower Came'

136 **childe:** a candidate for knighthood
137 **cockle:** a cornfield weed
calcine: burn to ashes
bents: coarse, dry grasses
139 **howlet:** owl
bespate: spattered with
140 **Apollyon:** (in the New Testament) the Greek name for the king of Hell
141 **nonce:** moment
start: burst apart
heft: hilt
slug-horn: horn used to sound a challenge

'De Gustibus–'

146 **Apennine:** Italian mountains
cicala: cicada, an insect like a grasshopper
drouth: drought
147 **the king:** for much of the time the Brownings lived there, Italy was a divided country, partly under the control of France. The Brownings supported the cause of Italian independence and unification, which was achieved in 1861, the year Elizabeth Barrett Browning died.
touched in the liver-wing: just grazed by the bullet
felons: criminals
Queen Mary: Mary Queen of Scots (1542–1587), who said that when she died 'Calais' would be found written on her heart, because she was so upset at losing the town to the French in 1558.

FURTHER READING

You will find the complete poems from which the extracts in *Three Victorian Poets* have been taken in these editions:

Herbert Warren & Frederick Page (eds), *Tennyson: Complete Poems and Plays* (Oxford University Press, 1953)

John Bolton & Julia Holloway (eds), *Elizabeth Barrett Browning: Aurora Leigh and Other Poems* (Penguin Classics, 1995)

Malcolm Hicks (ed.), *Elizabeth Barrett Browning: Selected Poems* (Carcanet, 1983)

Daniel Karlin (ed.), *Robert Browning: Selected Poetry* (Penguin Poetry Library, 1989)

Biographies and critical reading

Michael Thorn, *Tennyson* (Abacus, 1992)

Margaret Forster, *Elizabeth Barrett Browning* (Flamingo, 1988)

Betty Miller, *Robert Browning, A Portrait* (Penguin, 1952)

Christopher Ricks's *Tennyson* (Macmillan, 1989) is part biography and part criticism.

Marjorie Stone's *Elizabeth Barrett Browning* (Macmillan Women Writers Series, 1995) is a feminist re-reading of her work.

John Woolford & Daniel Karlin's *Robert Browning* (Longman, 1996) offers recent re-readings of the poet's work.

Ellen Moers, *Literary Women* (The Women's Press, 1978) and Joanna Russ, *How to Suppress Women's Writing* (The Women's Press, 1984) are both full of references to Elizabeth Barrett Browning, for readers who wish to pursue the ideas about writers' reputations, and the reasons why women writers sometimes 'disappear'.

Facts and fictions

Royston Pike (ed.), *Human Documents of the Industrial Revolution* (Unwin University Books, 1966). For people studying history as well as literature, these are first-hand accounts from adults and children, working in mines and factories between 1800 and 1850. A second volume, *Human Documents of the Victorian Golden Age* (1967), covers the second half of the nineteenth century.

For illustrated information about Victorian art and architecture, see:

Christopher Wood, *The Pre-Raphaelites* (Weidenfeld and Nicholson, 1981)

Roger Dixon & Stefan Muthesius, *Victorian Architecture* (Thames and Hudson, 1985)

Margaret Forster, *Lady's Maid* (Penguin, 1988) and Virginia Woolf, *Flush* (Penguin, 1977; first published 1933), are both biographical novels, the first about the life of Elizabeth Barrett Browning's maid, Wilson, and the second about her dog, Flush.

A. S. Byatt, *Possession* (Chatto and Windus, 1990): the novelist tells the story of two fictional Victorian poets, and also creates their poetical works, reflecting many of the ideas and themes common to Tennyson and the Brownings.

CAMBRIDGE LITERATURE

Ben Jonson   *The Alchemist*

William Wycherley   *The Country Wife*

Robert Burns   *Selected Poems*

William Blake   *Selected Works*

Jane Austen   *Pride and Prejudice*

Mary Shelley   *Frankenstein*

Three Victorian Poets

Charlotte Brontë   *Jane Eyre*

Emily Brontë   *Wuthering Heights*

Nathaniel Hawthorne   *The Scarlet Letter*

Charles Dickens   *Great Expectations*

George Eliot   *Silas Marner*

Henrik Ibsen   *A Doll's House*

Robert Louis Stevenson   *Treasure Island*

Mark Twain   *Huckleberry Finn*

Thomas Hardy   *Tess of the d'Urbervilles*

Oscar Wilde   *The Importance of Being Earnest*

Kate Chopin   *The Awakening and other stories*

Anton Chekhov   *The Cherry Orchard*

James Joyce *Dubliners*

Six Poets of the Great War

D. H. Lawrence *Selected Short Stories*

Edith Wharton *Ethan Frome*

Edith Wharton *The Age of Innocence*

Robert Cormier *After the First Death*

Fay Weldon *Letters to Alice*

Louise Lawrence *Children of the Dust*

Julian Barnes *A History of the World in 10½ Chapters*

Amy Tan *The Joy Luck Club*

Four Women Poets

Moments of Madness – *150 years of short stories*